The Academic Weight Room

[2016 Edition]

David Conarroe

Oakamoor
Publishing

For my Mom, Carolyn Conarroe, HS English teacher and author, and my Dad, Percy Conarroe, newspaper owner, honored journalist and prolific editorial writer.

Thanks to my wife Judy and sons Jeff and Andy for staying with me and encouraging me through my life-long professional journey in education and coaching.

About the Author

David Conarroe has been an educator and coach since 1976. His 35-year career in the secondary classroom as a teacher of business, IB Business and Management, IB Economics, AP Economics, and A-Level Business Studies in Northern Ireland included 10 years as high school athletic director and 25 years as head basketball coach. In 2012, he was hired on an interim basis by California State University, Bakersfield to stabilize and reinvent the athletics academic support center. Having accomplished that mission, he retired from CSUB in 2014. He currently is an academic support coach and consultant in support of the Academic Weight Room project.

Acknowledgements

This project would not have been possible without the help and encouragement from the following people:

Michael Woodrow for the assistance in getting the project started, especially all the technical help in getting the web page off the ground provided by the crew at Aspen Tech Labs

Carolyn Fields Popinchalk, retired teacher, for reading the first draft of the book and providing insight.

My editor James Lumsden-Cook at Bennion Kearny.

Victoria College Belfast Headmistress Margaret Anderson and all of my colleagues and friends at VCB, without whom this entire process would most likely not have begun.

Everyone at California State University, Bakersfield for their support before, during, and after my gig as the Athletics Academic Support Coach, but especially my office partner and fellow Athletics Academic Support Adviser Phyllis Wallace, Melissa Bowen, AD Ziggy Siegfried, former AD Jeff Konya, Associate AD Cindy Goodmon, Associate AD Karen Langston, Head Men's Basketball Coach Rod Barnes, Assistant Men's Basketball Coach Jeff Conarroe,

Head Women's Basketball Coach Greg McCall, Head Women's Soccer Coach Gary Curneen, Head Men's Soccer Coach Richie Grant, Swim Director Chris Hansen, Head Water Polo Coach Jason Gall, Head Wrestling Coach Mike Mendoza, Director of Track and Field and Cross Country Marcia Mansur-Wentworth, Head Softball Coach Chris Buck, Head Strength and Conditioning Coach Brendan Zeigler, Academic Advising and Resource Center director Jennifer McCune, AARC adviser April Thompson, CSUB President Dr. Horace Mitchell, Dean of Student Affairs Dr. Thomas Wallace, Dean of Enrollment Management Dr. Jacquelyn Mimms, Faculty Athletics Representative Dr. Jacquelyn Kegley, Faculty Athletics Representative Dr. Roy Lafever, Compliance Director Marcus Brown, colleague Nadine Griffith who came on board a few months after Phyllis and I got things going, and Dena Freeman Paton who was hired as the Associate AD for Academics in 2013 to lead the Kegley Center for Athletics Academic Support.

And of course, thanks to the thousands of students in my classrooms and workshops and the hundreds of athletes I coached who enabled this mutual educational experience. Without them none of this would have happened.

Table of Contents

Chapter 1
You Have Been Told What You Need to Do. But Do You Know Why and How?

Background story

The following quote by John Lachs, professor at Vanderbilt University, has informed my teaching and coaching efforts since it appeared in Nick Hartshorn's 1996 book *Catch: A Discovery of America*:

"The really important thing is not what people will remember you for, but what contribution have you made to their lives, such that they may not even remember you made it."

Recently, I was fortunate to spend lunch with student athlete with whom I worked at California State University, Bakersfield (CSUB). She recalled a suggestion, during my first term as academic support coach, on essay structure. At the time, she thought the advice was simple and because our interaction was so brief, she almost dismissed it (see Chapter 16 on essay structure). But she gave it a go. And she was amazed by the subsequent decline in her anxiety levels as she applied the strategy to papers, exam essay answers, and research papers for every course over the next three years.

I share this story because it captures the essence of the quote above; she told me I provided a skill which made a difference, but had we not spoken it is likely she would not have realized the difference it made. Indeed, I (almost imperceptibly to her) introduced a strategy which improved both her academic performance and quality of life.

Why how and why matters more than what

Almost every college student with whom I have interacted over the past three years has already heard what they are supposed to do to be a successful student; some have heard this advice so often they roll their eyes each time they hear it again. If they have been told what to do, then why do at least a third of the students in a typical school have academic problems? The answer is in this book; a book for students at the high school, college, and university level who would like to learn academic skills they were never taught or review skills they have now forgotten.

A little over 30 years into my teaching career, and several years after the revelation which occurred to me during my Fulbright year in Belfast (of which I will talk later), I came across a business management book by Simon Sinek, *Start With Why*. His thesis was that while business understands completely what they are doing/selling (and that is *what* they try to sell), consumers will respond better to the marketing effort if they understand *why* the business is doing what it does; any business can explain what it does, but few can explain why.

In his book, Sinek draws a diagram he calls the Golden Circle, with a small circle of *why* in the center, surrounded by a slightly larger circle of how, which is then surrounded by a large circle of what. He explains that business is stuck in the largest, most obvious, circle of what. The interesting thing to me was not necessarily the idea of starting with *why*, but that many teachers (like business) focus on *what* in the classroom as well, for the most part ignoring *why* and *how*.

As my teaching career started to wind down, it dawned on me that the *how* needed almost as much attention as the what. I have since discovered that very few high school teachers have the time or inclination to teach the *how* and *why*, mostly due to the constraints that a top-down curriculum dictates, assessment models requiring adherence to a set pedagogy and rubric, and the high-stakes testing which is driving the student's focus on answers and test results.

Indeed many students succeed in high school simply by memorizing material for the exam, learning strategies for successful scores on the ACT/SAT exams, adhering to rubrics and expectations, doing no more than required. While doing this, these students have not learned the process of learning and inherent critical thinking skills such as analysis and evaluation.

Early in my teaching career, an administrator told me, in an evaluation, that I taught too much like a coach. He let it sit there, as if I understood completely what he was talking about. I didn't. He made it seem that being a coach in a classroom was somehow bad, but I could simply not figure out what he meant. What he did not seem to understand was that coaches have to explain both the *why* and *how* as they teach the *what*.

As a coach, I utilized the IDEA model (Introduce, Demonstrate, Explain, Attend), which is/was part of the ASEP (American Sport Education Program) Coaching Certification course I taught when I was an athletic director. A good coach/teacher:

- Introduces the concept, skill, or technique by clearly and concisely saying what it is and why it is important before

- Demonstrating it, then

- Explaining in detail about it, and then

- Attending to the players as they practice, providing feedback to enable acquisition of the skill.

And as the academic support coach, I used this same model to teach the student athletes academic skills which they had forgotten or were never taught.

The website Edutopia has a plethora of research, articles, and blog posts designed to help educators become better. In April 2012, Dr. Richard Curwin posted a column, *Telling Isn't Teaching: The Fine Art of Coaching*, which further explains what I am talking about. He wrote, "Coaches understand that telling a player (or singer, actor, etc.) what to do is not enough. Coaches are fully aware that knowing what to do is not the same as knowing how to do it." And I think this statement resonates with my own observations the last two years. I know we have courses in place to tell the students what they need to be doing; I taught one of them. But I also know that when we tell the students that they need to study more, or work harder, or manage time better, they just roll their eyes.

You have probably been told what you need to be doing to be smarter, to be a better student. And you probably try to do what you think you are supposed to do. Sometimes, however, students simply misinterpret the instructions or simply don't understand how to accomplish the *what*. How often have you been told to spend two hours studying, only to use the entire two hours of dedicated time trying to get through a chapter? There is a better way to accomplish the 'manage your time' instruction.

Atule Gawande, in an article for *New Yorker Magazine* in 2011, wrote, "Good coaches know how to break down performance into its critical individual components."

The Academic Weight Room is a compilation of key academic skills which have been broken down into understandable and applicable chunks by your academic coach. Academic success requires hard work, organization, planning, mental toughness, and strategies which will improve both your efficiency and your effectiveness. Learning how to utilize the critical components of a successful student's academic infrastructure, explained in this book, will help you to meet those requirements and will enable you to better comprehend concepts and better demonstrate higher level thinking skills, such as analysis and evaluation.

I first put some of these strategies into practice as a college student and later as an IB and A-Level classroom teacher. But it was as the academic support coach at CSUB that I was able to bring to fruition this idea that academic skills infrastructure could be improved – that students could become smarter.

During that time, I discovered that as many as half of all students lacked one or more academic skills necessary to achieve at a higher level, skills that professors generally expect students to have already mastered. It is this student need that pushed me to develop the sessions where I strengthened each student in one or more components of academic infrastructure. This book is a collection of the sessions and the stories that led to each skill set. All strategies have been updated to reflect the most recent research on learning.

Education is a process which requires you to proactively involve yourself in all phases in the same way that an athlete is immersed in the culture and expectations of his/her sport and team. As a teacher, I spoke to my classes in much the same way I spoke to my players, introducing, demonstrating, explaining, and then attending to the practice as they learned. And as the academic support coach, I spoke to my student athletes as a teacher, explaining how to do things rather than simply telling them what to do.

As a coach, I loved the pre-game speech. These gatherings were motivational in nature, designed to focus the players' attention on the demands of the upcoming challenge. We used the time to focus our energy on the things we could control and not to worry about those we could not. We reviewed our goals and objectives for the event, and reminded ourselves how it would be possible to emerge victorious. We generally ended with a key phrase or word to channel our energy toward a positive result.

It is much the same in the world of academic support. The 'opponent' is the course, the professor, the exam, and the score is your grade. Most obstacles to success will be internal, things that you are able to control and/or change as needed. Your skills infrastructure can be changed and improved.

So let's get this started. Huddle up, put a hand in, and repeat our key phrase: "Process is intelligence getting to know itself."

On three. One, two, three. Let's go.

Chapter 2
Why and How You can Become Smarter

- What is an academic skill?

- Is being 'smart' an ability or a skill?

- What is the difference between ability, capability, and skill?

- How can you improve your academic skill set?

Background story

As the academic support coach at California State University, Bakersfield, (CSUB), I provided a wide range of support services for our student athletes. A number of our athletes achieved fine grades and their classroom performance was exemplary – so I never saw them. However, for most, I either supervised them in study hall or met with them during individual appointments.

Early on, a couple of softball players who did poorly on one of the first quizzes came to my office to ask if I knew anything about physiology. I said, no, but that I could help. This was unexpected for the students since the norm is still to get a tutor in that specific class.

Instead, I talked to them about their routines before a class, during class, and after class. Like most students, they had some idea of what to do, but simply were not doing what was needed because they did not have a clear picture of how to do it. So I asked them to do the three steps of the pre-class routine I called BC, and the three steps of the 'during class' routine I called DC, and come back the next day to show me what they had done.

At that meeting, we reviewed the routine, compared their results, and I explained to them the after class routine called AC, which I asked them to undertake for the next seven days. Then, if progress was not being made we would secure a physiology tutor. It turned out, after seven days, that they didn't need the tutor after all. They just needed academic skills infrastructure strengthening

A combination of too many students needing this kind of help, coupled with limited resources to actually hire enough tutors to meet with every student who wanted one, necessitated a complementary strategy. And our needs were exacerbated by my anecdotal observation that at least a third of the students admitted to CSUB with the necessary GPA lacked sufficient academic skills infrastructure to achieve at a successful level in class. This observation is in no way an indictment of the admission standards of CSUB. Students with above average high school GPA and entrance exam scores sometimes struggled in one or more courses. I suggest this trend is a function of our K-12 emphasis on testing, and pushing students and parents to focus on grades rather than learning; answers rather than process. Thus the Academic Weight Room was born for our student athletes and soon it was made available to the entire student population on campus through the Academic Advising and Resource Center.

How do you improve your academic skill set?

The Academic Weight Room brings you strategies developed by a former teacher and academic support coach for learning academic skills you were never taught, or to refresh those academic skills you have forgotten. As you improve your academic skill infrastructure, you will improve academic performance.

When the student embraces the process rather than focuses on outcomes, the results, or the answers – he/she begins to grow as a learner.

You can improve your academic skill the same way an athlete working with a coach improves her/his athletic skill.

Myelin is an insulating sheath around neurons in the nervous system that enables faster firings. Athletes have more myelin wrap in particular nodes around skills like jumping or quickness or hitting a baseball than non-athletes. The same thing occurs with an academic skill; just as an athlete can become bigger, faster, or stronger by regularly participating in fitness training, so can a student become 'smarter' by embracing the process of learning. Think of the Academic Weight Room as a toolbox which helps you to develop the skills necessary to think critically rather than memorize as many answers as possible.

Abilities

During my career as basketball coach and athletic director, I was a certified instructor for Coaching and Sport First Aid courses through ASEP (American Sport Education Program) through Human Kinetics. One of my core texts was Spor*t Skill Instruction for Coaches by* Craig Wrisberg; he defines abilities as relatively permanent and includes speech, sight, hearing, taste, and memory.

These abilities are genetically determined characteristics that are relatively stable and which dictate to some extent the athlete's potential for performance. As I have said, for years, to both students in my classes and players on my teams – each of us has a genetic threshold and we must try to push to the top edge of that threshold.

I submit that students who are smart are not just resting on their genetic ability (which is what it looks like to many other students who are struggling academically) but instead are combining that native ability, or intelligence, with learned skills to push to the upper reaches of their genetic threshold.

Wrisberg differentiates between ability, capability, and skill, even though these terms seem to be used interchangeably. Capabilities are similar to abilities, but can be improved with practice. A skill is the athlete's current level of proficiency on a given task; this task is a function of ability and capability plus experience and practice. An athlete with skill can execute a given task in a proficient manner.

We can improve both capability and skill through purposeful practice and routine, similar to the way coaches help athletes improve in their sport.

Wrisberg added, "The challenge for the coach is to create practice experiences [opportunities] that allow [student] athletes to maximize their abilities, improve their capabilities, and develop skills needed to achieve the best performance possible."

Chapter 2

During my time as the Athletics Academic Support Coach at CSUB, I heard more than one professor state that a student 'didn't belong' or 'wasn't smart enough' to be on his/her course. A student gets admitted to a university because they pass academic admission criteria. But once admitted for attendance, the student sometimes finds her/himself treading water at best, or drowning at worst. It is simply wrong to blame that student since they were fairly granted admission; instead we should focus on why he/she is struggling and figure out a way to throw them a lifeline to enable them to perform. I contend that it is not Wrisberg's definition of ability, or native intelligence, that is the issue – which is what the professors implied – but rather insufficient academic skill set. In fairness to the professors, perhaps the terms used needed further clarification (as Wrisberg did in his book).

It is clear that the students in the story that opened this chapter came to the course with the ability to perform, and it is clear that they held the necessary credentials to belong in school. It is also clear that the academic skills they developed improved their performance and their capability to succeed in subsequent courses. In short, the academic skill they gained made them smarter.

The difference between ability and capability is marginal, and many tend to use the terms interchangeably. The point of this discussion is to recognize that all students have the ability to learn additional skills which will then provide the capability to perform in future courses. It is my belief that an academic skill is an ability which can be improved and this improvement makes you smarter. In the end, smart is a function of genetic threshold, or innate talent, combined with learned skill.

Chapter 3
Process is Intelligence
Getting to Know Itself

To be a better student, embrace the process rather than focus on the product.

Background story

I was a Fulbright exchange teacher at Victoria College Belfast, Northern Ireland, in 2001-2002. As a teacher of A-Level business studies, I was charged with helping 35 students get an exam score that would get them into the university of their choice.

According to my students, the generally accepted model of instruction at VCB seemed to be for the instructor to go over the text after the students had read it, lecturing almost verbatim whilst they then took notes. Then they would re-read the text and re-read the notes and the instructor would provide answers to problems before moving on to the next unit. Right away, the students were in for a little shock as I tried to get them to adopt my process model rather than the more accepted focus on results and answers.

One day, in a review session for the particular unit, I showed the students what I was trying to get them to do: break down the question they had never seen before and arrive at a solution. Most found this to be very difficult; evidently, they had not been asked, in any of their classes, to use their content retention and comprehension to figure out an answer to a question.

Instead, in preparation for this very important A-Level exam, they wanted 'the answer' to the question they had never seen before so they could memorize it. One student, Miss C, was asked if she could explain the question; asked how to demonstrate her thinking process and how she would arrive at the answer. After studying the question for a minute or so, she said, "Mr. Conarroe, I could not possibly know the answer to this question as I have never seen it before."

I stuck with the process focus. Some students embraced process while others stuck with their tried and true focus on answers and results. While some embraced process, others were not so sure. Indeed, one student was so convinced that I had totally ruined her chance at university that she simply wanted to drop the course and not take that exam. She reasoned that three good scores in her other subjects would suffice but that a poor score in one of four might hurt. I spent significant time reassuring her that she was doing fine, that the process would work. In the end, she stayed in the class, took the exam, and achieved her highest exam score in my class.

Later that spring, another anecdotal piece of support for my process thesis was presented through a letter to the editor of the *Belfast Telegraph* newspaper. A daily ritual for staff was morning tea when everyone gathered in the staff workroom for tea, snacks, and small talk. On this particular day, I noticed three or four very upset English teachers, around a table, in animated conversation about a letter in the morning newspaper. One was crying, as she was certain her firing was imminent. Curiosity aroused, I went over to the group to find out what was happening.

The A-Level English students had just finished their exams and according to the letter writer, VCB had ruined one student's life because the English teachers had failed to teach her about a poem the exam required the students to analyze. In fact, the student evidently had never even seen this poem before, so how could she possibly understand, interpret, analyze, and evaluate it?

According to the letter writer, the student's failure to handle one portion of the A-Level English exam was surely going to keep the student out of a competitive university, relegating her to a less desirable school, ostensibly ruining her life. Of course, I could not refrain from stepping in to offer my observations, as this was exactly what I had been pondering. (Not the poetry of course, but process versus answer.) I asked them if it was possible for them to possibly teach their students about every possible poem written by every English and Irish poet? Of course not. The whole idea of the exam was to test whether the students could read poetry and figure out what the poet was talking about; doing this is a process that is taught, a skill that is learned. They were not at all calmed by my reasoning, but I did have a conversation with the headmistress about this issue and the conversation led to a presentation to the staff about process.

I doubt I changed many minds; one teacher told me that it would be blasphemous to suggest to parents that process trumps results, but the event catalyzed my thinking, and eventually evolved into the Academic Weight Room.

What is process?

Learning is constructed, not received from the professor. This construction requires you to involve yourself in a process of learning. This process is a struggle, simply because you are unlikely to already know everything that a course is trying to teach you.

This struggle comes as a surprise to many students who look around and conclude that education is supposed to be easy, and they look for strategies to make that move to Easy Street. What they might not have discovered is that many students, for whom the process of education seems easy, have embraced the process of learning and accompanying strategies to enhance that learning process. This process includes memorization, but memorization alone is not learning. Learning involves reading, writing, the application of content knowledge, and critical thinking skills, which involve problem solving, analysis, and evaluation.

The aphorism "Process is Intelligence Getting to Know Itself" comes from Robert Fripp and serves as the driving philosophy of the entire AWR idea. This aphorism, aligning with Carol Dweck's thesis in *Mindset*, suggests that intelligence is not fixed, but rather grows via the engagement of process.

In my high school business classes, I defined process as the activities by the business which produced a product or service. In business, it is absolutely necessary to go through a process every day in an effort to provide goods and services which meet the needs of the customer.

In my graduate program at Northern Arizona University, I learned that writing is a process rather than a product. Indeed, my graduate-level English Composition course was a daily process of writing, editing and rewriting (in longhand) until I could show an acceptable proficiency in writing to my professor. Over that 15-week semester, I learned the habits and actions required of writers, coming to understand what Barbara Oakley says in her book *A Mind for Numbers: How to Excel at Math and Science, Even if you Flunked Algebra,* "Process means the flow of time and the habits and actions associated with that flow of time. Product is the outcome." Merriam Webster's definition of process is also applicable: "a series of actions that lead to a particular result."

We want students to embrace the process, to have a focus on that series of actions that strengthen their core academic skill set. A focus on the process will enable incremental improvement, which will then bring about the desired results, as well as enhancing subsequent success in other classes. Of course, therein lies the rub: students have grown to understand that the answer is the most important thing, that the results matter, and that success lies in getting those desired results as quickly and effortlessly as possible. The process is a longer-term proposition which requires more focus, attention, and work. But, through process, the results are genuine and longer-lived.

Why the process model is better

Some students (and their advocates) pursue a results model and depend on tutors to get them through a course. This is a short-term solution, as many times the student has learned just enough to pass, but has not developed sufficient understanding or the prerequisite skill needed for a subsequent class in that discipline. Indeed, without a solid understanding of content coupled with the fundamental problem solving skills of application, analysis, and evaluation, a student will be crippled if/when he/she takes the next course in the sequence. A focus on results often means that subsequent results are inferior; which can initiate a downward spiral of hopeless resignation. The student begins to think, 'I am not smart enough.' The results model invariable involves memorizing answers or solutions, and often this is what tutors and teachers have the students accomplish. There is nothing wrong with using old tests to help prepare if the test is used to figure out what concepts might be covered and how the test question is structured; the old exam is used to help the student figure things out, but the answers to those questions should not be memorized. To summarize what Peter Brown (et al) says in his book *Make It Stick*, the problem with memorizing solutions or answers is the same as my student encountered in my opening example: what if the answer to the question you have memorized does not match the question you have been presented with?

The purpose of education and exams

The point of education is not simply to get students to memorize content, but to teach them how to learn, to explore mysterious subjects, to process new concepts, and to be exposed to different ideas about how things work. Educators generally strive to teach students 'how to think' rather than 'what to think', although this is being challenged by an increasing emphasis on standardized testing at all grade levels.

Exams in the classroom are most valuable to the education process when they are designed to get the student to think critically, which includes application, analysis, evaluation, and creativity.

Unfortunately, we seem to have reached a point where exams seem to be more about the answer to the question than the educational process. Still, most teachers and professors utilize pre-tests and post-tests along with formative assessments to mark progress in learning, and summative assessments to measure how well the student measures up to the standards of the course. While many utilize multiple-choice exams for formative assessments, most teachers will try to have a summative assessment using a format besides multiple choice which measures critical thinking skills as well as content knowledge.

There are four components to most examination questions: The examiner will expect the student to demonstrate **knowledge**, an understanding of content; evidence that the student has 'learned' the term, concept, or idea. This requires memorization, or the ability to recall that information. The command terms for this include define, describe, and explain. A question of this type requires a lower level thinking skill, and most exam questions include or imply this expectation.

The examiner will also expect the student to demonstrate a skill in **application,** which requires the student to demonstrate the ability to use appropriate graphs, formulae, diagrams which are drawn and/or used to arrive at a solution, and to connect the content to solution. This requires understanding, which is a combination of recall and comprehension.

The examiner, generally, would then expect the student to demonstrate skill in **analysis**, which is where and when the student

15

explains why and how something works, operates, interacts. It is a demonstration and understanding of the cause and effect relationships inherent in the question, case, problem, and the subsequent solution offered by the student. This is the first step in demonstrating recall, comprehension, AND critical thinking.

Finally, the examiner will generally (explicitly or implicitly) expect evidence of a skill in **evaluation**, which is the highest order critical thinking skill a student can develop and demonstrate. Evaluation includes more than a conclusion or opinion, but rather is an analysis and explanation of different sides of an argument, or the pro/con effects of the solution, with a reasoned conclusion based on how the evidence weighs up.

Process involves practice

Academic skills such as those we are teaching in the Academic Weight Room can be developed through practice. As Geoff Colvin says in his book *Talent is Overrated*, "extensive, well-structured, deliberate practice…can alter the physical nature of a person's brain and body."

The process of learning, or becoming a better athlete, or becoming a better musician, or improving talent in any skill, including academic skill, is a function of millions of brain cells called neurons, each of which contains a soma (which is sort of the heart of the neuron) a dendrite, an axon, and a terminal. Knowledge is embedded and skills are learned by creating neurotransmitter pathways which connect these neurons in unique ways to other neurons, enabling the recall or utilization of that particular skill. The key to the pathway (that the electrical impulses called neurotransmitters utilize) is the axon, which is wrapped with a substance (mentioned in Chapter 2) called myelin.

As a particular neurotransmitter pathway is used, myelin is wrapped around that axon, strengthening that neurotransmission. The more wrapping that occurs, the stronger that signal or strength. This continues until the skill becomes an instinct and the knowledge becomes part of your day-to-day living.

So how do you 'wrap' myelin? You pursue a process Colvin calls "deliberate practice." He says, "We are wrong to think that the exceptional nature of great performance is a pre-ordained outcome.

It is, rather, a result of a process, the general elements of which are clear."

The Academic Weight Room is all about this process of strengthening those neurotransmitter pathways; you become smarter by utilizing specific techniques and practicing particular skills. This is why the research done by Peter Brown et al, reported in *Make It Stick*, proves that you can become 'smarter'. Learning is a process of building those neurotransmitter pathways and wrapping the myelin; the more usage, the more myelin and the more myelin, the stronger that neurotransmission and the more you know and the more talented you seem to others.

Brown says that memory is improved when you utilize two techniques which stress your neurotransmitter delivery system and force a stronger myelin wrap. They recommend *interleaving*, which is studying or practicing many different things during the course of a practice or study session. And they recommend spacing, which is coming back to the skill or information a day or two later, then a couple of days after that, then a week or so after that. *AC: The After Class Study Routine* addresses these ideas. And the unfortunate truth is that these intellectual and academic strengths decay in the same way that physical strengths decay if they are not maintained, and used, via repetition over time.

An example of process

How many of you have been given an assignment to do a research paper? When I asked this question of students in a recent AWR session, I was surprised by the number of hands that didn't go up. Asking again, the number of students who had NOT been assigned a research paper was still near 10% of the group. That must be some indication that the pressure to prepare for various standardized exams is forcing teachers to give up what used to be a normal part of the education process in 10th grade, or sooner.

Still, it is very likely most students have been taught the research paper process in high school. It is also likely that many students focused on getting the research paper 'done', with a 'good' grade, rather than understanding the purpose of the paper in the first place. The point of the research paper at high school level is to teach the process, but the student might have interpreted the point as learning more about the topic or (more likely) simply as work that needed to be completed and accomplished.

How to embrace the process

Think back to the story at the beginning of this chapter and the student who did poorly on the exam question requiring her to break down a poem to arrive at answers and an interpretation. When she approached her exam preparation as a series of questions that had correct answers that she could memorize, she necessarily limited her knowledge to a set of answers. If she had embraced process, and paid attention when the teacher showed her how to break down a poem to arrive at an interpretation and possible answers to questions, she would have been able to use that skill to break down ANY poem she came across.

Accomplishing anything requires you to go through a series of steps, each of which need to be achieved before you move to the next. Jay Bilas reminds us, in his book *Toughness,* "You can't get to the top of the ladder in one step." The process of going up a ladder one step at a time is incremental progress. Sometimes these small steps, or incremental gains, are so small that we don't notice them or we take them for granted, especially as we approach proficiency in that particular step.

At other times, the process (or ladder) seems too daunting. If the journey up the ladder is worthwhile, you simply must take a step, then another, then another, embracing that process rather than focusing on the end result. Soon, the process will culminate in your desired result. However, some people think there is a shortcut to the top of the ladder. There isn't. But there is a shortcut to the bottom of the ladder; Bilas reminds us it takes only one step to get there!

A process (as a noun) is the collection of the steps you take to accomplish something; it is an understanding of the parts involved in an action so you can go through each part or step necessary to accomplish that action.

To process (as a verb) something is to make sense of it, to extract meaning from something, to see the interconnected, cause and effect relationships of the interactive parts of the process. Whether you embrace the process (noun) by undertaking each of the steps from beginning to end, or process (verb) what is happening… you are gaining intelligence.

In each case, you are breaking the action down into integral parts which generally have to be completed in a particular order. As you go through the process more than once, each time you complete the process, it becomes easier, until you gain an expert level understanding or ability. What you process, you learn; when you go through a process, you learn. Again, back to our mantra: Process is intelligence getting to know itself.

Those who focus on results tend to overlook or ignore the reality of those incremental steps crucial to the attainment of the result, thinking instead that an illusory shortcut will be the ticket to success. Athletes who report to a strength and conditioning coach to become incrementally bigger, faster, and stronger are embracing a process. Students who embrace process by learning and practicing the strategies, techniques, and skills in this book will also become stronger academically and will see long term gains in academic performance.

Chapter 4
To Become Smarter,
Embrace a Growth
Mindset

My hometown has a yearly gathering of researchers, writers, intellectuals, educators, and curiosity seekers. It's called The Aspen Ideas Festival and was founded in 2005.

Once, I was fortunate enough to spend an evening with Dr. Carol Dweck of Stanford during which she presented research she had just completed and which was subsequently released in her book *Mindset*.

While I was not aware of her theory and research on mindset, I did embrace a similar idea credited many years earlier to Henry Ford: "Whether you think you can, or think you can't, you are right."

What Dweck quantified in her research is that people generally are one of two mindsets: fixed, or growth, and that to learn in an academic setting, a growth mindset is crucial. Indeed, what she said that night immediately made sense. Students whom I felt had the potential to do well on the course sometimes did not even try, thinking they were not 'smart enough' and others looked to drop the course soon after the first graded exam because they deemed it 'too hard.' These reactions are typical of students with a fixed mindset, so it was apparent that I needed to address that perception and nudge them towards the growth mindset.

In one of my pre-AWR mindset sessions during class, in the early days of my IB courses, the students on my course became involved in a conversation about a particularly talented and intelligent student who went on to MIT and who had achieved the highest score possible in IB (a seven) a year earlier. The consensus was that this student was simply 'smart' and that the students discussing him were 'not smart.'

In conversation with the MIT student the summer following the exam, I learned that one of reasons behind his ability/ intelligence/ high score had more to do with what happened before, during, and after class than innate intelligence. The student was smart, no doubt, but he felt he did more 'studying' than most, and wanted me to know that the score was a function of a growth mindset, or a belief that growth and improvement is possible.

He also pointed out how many people who were not 'smart' could become 'smarter' but they typically exhibited a 'fixed' mindset in which they simply went to class, listened, took a few notes, then crammed for the exams.

What is mindset?

According to Brown et al, in their book *Make It Stick*, what matters most in content and knowledge acquisition is mindset, language fluency, reading ability, and a willingness to engage in active learning in order to distill underlying principles and build structure.

In turn, learning styles don't matter.

Mindset is the first, perhaps most important, characteristic mentioned. Indeed, in my experience as a teacher and coach, I have found the first obstacle many students must overcome is simply the fixed mindset. As Carol Dweck wrote in *Mindsets: Developing Talent Through a Growth Mindset* (written for coaches of US Olympic athletes) "Research has shown repeatedly that teaching students the growth mindset strongly enhances their motivation and their achievement."

Those with a fixed mindset think that talent is given, or fixed, and no matter what they do, that talent is limited to what exists. Those with fixed mindsets believe that natural abilities are the only key to success, that talent matters more than effort, toughness, drive; that a safe win is better than a possible loss and that academic and athletic challenges are to be avoided. But most damagingly, a fixed mindset leads one to be afraid of failure and averts opportunities to learn and do better next time.

A growth mindset, on the other hand, sees people think that talent, skills, and abilities can be developed, or grown, with instruction and through determined practice and hard work.

According to Dweck, not everyone has the same potential, but everyone has potential, and those with a growth mindset do what is possible to develop and grow that potential.

In the article to Olympic coaches, quoted above, Dweck identifies three rules all students, coaches and teachers need to understand about fixed vs growth mindsets. "In a fixed mindset the cardinal rule is: Look talented at all costs. In a growth mindset, the cardinal rule is: Learn, learn, learn.

"In a fixed mindset, the second rule is: Don't work too hard or practice too much. In a growth mindset, the rule is: Work with passion and dedication – effort is the key.

"In a fixed mindset, the third rule is: When faced with setbacks, run away or conceal your deficiencies. In a growth mindset, the rule is: Embrace your mistakes and confront your deficiencies."

Dweck goes on to say that, "a growth mindset allows each player to embrace learning, to welcome challenges, mistakes, and feedback, and to understand the role of effort in creating talent. [And] when coaching staff have a fixed mindset, their job is simply to find talent. When they have a growth mindset, their job is to inspire and promote the development of talent."

How to create the 'growth mindset'

Embracing a growth mindset is a process that takes attentive effort. It requires an awareness of your current thought processes and a conscious engagement of 'growth' thoughts. A growth mindset can be learned, developed, and assimilated *if* you pay attention to words and actions that drive behaviors. It is important to understand that it is not enough to simply believe; you must act on that belief.

Choose the growth path that is on the right-hand side, next. It has been adapted from a diagram by Nigel Holmes (in the same article written for the Olympic coaches) and examines a person's thinking filtered through both the fixed and the growth mindset:

Fixed	Growth
Intelligence is fixed	Intelligence can be developed
Hard = Not smart enough	Hard = Can figure it out
Hard = Find an easier way	Hard = Get to work
Want to look smart	Want to learn
Avoid challenges	Embrace challenges
Don't even try if might lose	Losing is part of process
Give up early when facing obstacles	Persist in face of setback
Effort is useless; only talent matters	Effort is path to mastery
Constructive criticism is negative	Learn from criticism
Offended by negative feedback	Criticism not taken personally
Threatened by other's success	Find lessons in other's success
Achieve less than full potential	Higher level of achievement
Can't fail if don't try.	Can't win if don't try.

Why does the growth mindset matter?

Recruiters are paying attention. A Venn diagram called *Attracting and Retaining Top Talent*, developed by Andrew Miller of ACM Consulting, helps us to understand the intersection of mindset, attitude, and skill in our educational, athletic, and career journeys.

Key Attributes of Top Talent

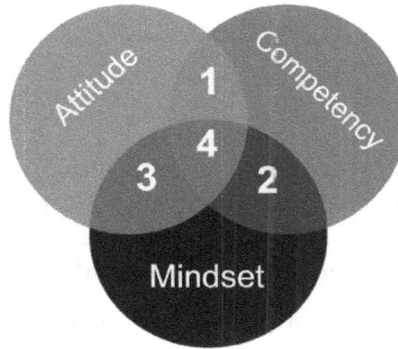

[Reproduced with permission]

Every student being considered for admission by a university, every prospect being recruited by a coach, or every candidate being considered by HR for a job will have characteristics the organization looks for in each of the three circles above. These three areas represent attitude, mindset, and competency; skills which will add value to the organization.

People who have only the attitude and skill circles which intersect at 1 will have a productive attitude and a value-added skillset, but have a fixed mindset which will limit their progress. People who have only mindset and attitude circles (which intersect at 3) are great to have on the team, but don't add value (which leads to a net loss in productivity).

People who have the growth mindset and skill circles which intersect at 2 offer value and the most desirable mindset, but will be selfish and tend to show no loyalty to the team/organization which reduces their long-term viability. The ideal student, athlete, or employee for recruiters, coaches and HR will be the person whose three attribute circles intersect at 4.

You want to put yourself in that sweet spot where all three attributes of success intersect. You want to put yourself into a position where you have a chance to develop the most beneficial personal traits for each circle. A growth mindset and productive attitude help you to utilize the entire educational process to learn not only a vocational skill, but also academic and problem solving skills, including critical thinking and creativity. You *can* be the person who is recruited over others, ultimately.

Summary

This chapter showed you how to adopt a growth mindset. The entire premise of Dweck's research is that you can learn, you can develop talent, you can become smarter, you can take advantage of your potential and move towards the upper end of your genetic threshold.

A growth mindset is what gives you the impetus to move forward, to accept challenges, to learn from defeat, to embrace the process, while a fixed mindset mires you in your current situation, your current skill set. A growth mindset gives you the pathway for learning any skill and once that happens, offers a better chance at getting hired or recruited. It puts you in position to have a chance at some success, because you are willing to try. You decide; and how you subsequently act on that decision is a function of attitude.

The above diagram shows why a productive attitude is also crucial to your long-term success. But sometimes we fixate only on skills, thinking that is all we need. The next chapter explains how to recognize and develop a productive attitude. A productive attitude will motivate you to engage in any sort of activity or performance.

Chapter 5
Handling the Rigor of the University Academic Experience

The Professor said "work harder"

One of my student athletes was having a difficult time on his first calculus course. Before arranging a tutor for him, I reviewed the process-oriented AWR strategies and routines before, during and after class. Then I suggested that he reach out to the professor during office hours since it was still early in the term. I encouraged him to be prepared for the meeting, to ask the professor for specific help on a specific problem he was having trouble with, as it would do no good for him to simply say, "I don't understand."

Supported by that strategy, he met with the professor. Instead of offering any sort of specific additional help for this particular concept, the professor said "Work Harder."

When we next met, I asked the student how his meeting went. "I am not sure. I didn't get the help I asked for. Instead, he told me to work harder. What exactly does he mean by work harder? I am going to class and spending at least two hours a day studying for this course."

What does the professor mean by 'work harder'?

Coach Jim Valvano, who led an underdog, outmanned North Carolina State basketball team to the national title in 1983, told me once at a coaching clinic that he did not stress offense and defense, he stressed hard work. He said that you might work hard and not win, but it is unlikely you can win without hard work. While some other teams might have enough talent to walk on the floor and win without seeming to work hard, his teams simply were not good enough to get by without hard work so he spent significant time teaching the concept of hard work. He repeatedly sent the message that hard work was about mindset; it's about grinding through and sticking with the process, including the fundamentals and seemingly insignificant details.

Success in school requires hard work. Education, especially at the university level, is supposed to be challenging. Indeed, I heard at an IB training this aphorism: Without struggle there is no gain, no learning, and the sooner you understand this – the more progress you will make.

Many students have a misconception that because school is easy for some students, it should be easy for everyone. Indeed, some students seem to be able to handle the course, the difficulty, the requirements without showing much effort. While it could be that the student is a genius with photographic memory, it is unlikely since there are so few of those. These students are likely utilizing a native talent or intelligence coupled with a system of study before, during and after class, enabled by learned academic skills, which makes things look easier than they are.

Most students tell me they understand the need to work hard, the need to manage time, the need to spend two hours per day per class in study mode. They have heard the 'what to do' before, but what seems to be lacking in that instruction is an understanding of what exactly each means and how to put each 'what' into productive use.

According to Dr. Tom Tutko, Professor Emeritus at San Jose State and arguably the guru of sport psychology, successful students and athletes demonstrate an ability to work harder than most people.

These successful students and athletes stick with their goals, schedule, study routine, and training regime regardless of the distractions. Results gained through hard work in any rigorous endeavor develop a person's self-esteem, which then feeds the belief that achieving a goal is possible, enabling an emotional drive and passion for the process.

With that being said, Scott Adams, in his book *How to Fail at Almost Everything and Still Win Big*, says we must be wary of passion; what often happens is that passion is stoked when things are going well, but tends to ebb if things are not going so well.

When you depend on passion, you will often be less committed when the going gets tough. He recommends, instead, a willingness to grind. Grinding requires energy, a willingness to stick with something, push through even if you seem to have lost the passion for it. Hard work is not only about the amount of time committed to the endeavor, but it is about how that time is spent, productively driven by grit and a growth mindset.

To answer my student's question from above, I shared several thoughts. First of all, it is not a matter of putting in more sleepless nights, clenching your jaw, gritting your teeth, and squinting. What the professor probably means is more likely an economic understanding of productivity related to hard work.

We need to improve our productivity, or increased output per hour of input, rather than just increasing our hours worked, hoping to see an improvement in our output. What you are looking for instead is a focus, a willingness to engage and commit to a reasonable time investment. When you work hard, you apply yourself to predetermined routines that have been proven to provide results.

Hard work requires you to apply the strategies and routines designed to organize daily activity and engagement on a regular and timely basis, which will improve the efficiency of that time spent. Sometimes time spent equates to hard work, but time alone is not an effective measure and it is not enough to simply 'put in the time.' Hard work is an output of effort and an investment of time.

As a coach, I am a student of other coaches, looking for words of advice and inspiration. Phil Jackson, with an NBA championship ring for every finger on his hand, is a particularly worthy coach to study. In his book *Sacred Hoops*, he has a chapter – "Being Aware is More Important than Being Smart" – in which he talks about how he taught his players to be in the present, to be completely aware of what is happening right now. By paying attention, the player is able to perform at the highest level, without self-talk and extraneous thoughts getting in the way.

According to Coach Jackson, enlightenment is achieved when, according to the teachings of Zen, we "chop wood, carry water." The point of this instruction, according to Jackson, is to "perform every activity, from playing basketball to taking out the garbage, with precise attention, moment by moment."

This led me to think about Van Morrison's song *Enlightenment*, in which he says, "Chop that wood. Carry water. What's the sound of one hand clapping? Enlightenment, don't know what it is." With these lyrics, he suggests that enlightenment is a mystery to him, but later in the same song he offers an answer when says, "It's up to you, the way you think. You're making your own reality every day."

Your success starts with your attitude

One of my colleagues at CSUB told me how discouraging she finds it to work with struggling students who don't seem to want to be there, who don't care. Perhaps their situation is learned helplessness, due to a lack of academic skills that would enable higher levels of performance. But maybe they have just lost interest; evidently they have stopped being present, they have lost focus. The simple reality is that 'what you are thinking' about the situation you are in will drive your behavior. If you don't really want to be here, you cannot possibly learn.

AMPS

All success is a function of Attitude, which enables intrinsic Motivation, which energizes the Performance leading to Success.

The AMPS building-block model to athletic and academic success was presented by another coach to whom I listened – at a coaching clinic – back in the late 70s or early 80s and to whom I apologize for not being able to cite 30+ years later.

At the time, it seemed to be such a simple but empowering message to share with my students and athletes. And from that point forward, it became a mantra for my classroom and teams. The simple guidance of AMPS was so powerful that one of my players wrote her college admissions essay about the concept, and how valuable it had become in her daily life. We used AMPS to break every huddle as a gentle reminder that we all needed to stay in the moment, purposefully attending to the situation at hand, doing the best we could with what we had.

One of the parents came up after a game and asked why we said 'Ants' after every huddle. I laughed and explained what we were actually saying and what it meant. He then laughed. He thought ants worked as well, as it seemed to represent our work ethic; that we were a team without a superstar, each sharing the workload without complaint, doing our part for the greater good without expectation of individual reward. Hmmm, that's also appropriate.

The dictionary defines attitude as a settled way of thinking or feeling about someone or something, typically one that is reflected in a person's behavior. Therefore, everything is a function of your attitude. Willingness to be here now, to participate, to embrace the process, to be coachable is a function of attitude; indeed, a coach would consider someone who demonstrates those characteristics to have a productive attitude.

First, you have to decide that you want to be in school to get an education. It is your attitude that determines whether you really want to learn how to think, to be better prepared for a career. There is a discrepancy that has to be confronted if you say you want to go to university, but then demonstrate you would rather be somewhere else with poor performance. And for athletes who simply want to get to the next level, you must realize that the purpose of most university programs is to provide an education while you see if you have what it takes to make the next level happen. For most, the next athletic level simply does not happen and the education becomes crucial. Therefore, it is imperative for you to strive to achieve.

Success in higher education is a function of reading ability, hard work, persistence, organization, preparation, and to a small extent, your native intelligence; most of these characteristics are clearly within your control, but if you really don't want to be here, the entire process is a waste of time for you. It is your attitude, which is reflected in your body language, which tells the coach, the academic support adviser, the professor, and your peers whether you are engaged or pretending. Pretenders cost money, are a bad investment, and are generally not worthy of further attention. Only you can decide if you want to do something; your decision is reflected in your attitude.

Chapter 5

Attitude enables motivation

With a good attitude, you are motivated. When you are motivated, you challenge yourself to perform to the best of your ability. If you perform to the best of your ability, you are successful. It is the basis from which you build your resume, your grade point average, your standing in school, and your standing on the team.

Attitude enables you to commit to your own cause, your own coach, your own team; if you commit to your own success and give everything that you have to this cause, you will find satisfaction. This is similar to the exhortation "no regrets" which is a mantra to remind you to be all in, whether it is in the gym or in the classroom.

You cannot get what you want in life with a lousy attitude. Without an appropriate attitude, you will have trouble finding success as a person. Everything begins with the appropriate attitude, because attitude enables motivation, which is the desire to do something.

Motivation is the determining factor in school, or your sport, for just about anything you choose to undertake, and whether that is an enjoyable experience for you. It is easy to stay motivated when things are going well; it is when things are not going your way that you need to dig deep and stay the course.

Internal or intrinsic motivation is what you decide to do to continue to be engaged, to be committed, to stay the course, regardless of the circumstances. External or extrinsic motivation comes from someone else (authority, coach, teacher, parent) in the form of either rewards or punishment based on your response to their directions. If you do something because you are afraid of the punishment or embarrassment you will suffer if you don't, you are being extrinsically motivated. If you do something because the want to do it, you enjoy doing it, or you expect to grow from the experience, you are experiencing intrinsic motivation.

Extrinsic motivation is effective only for a short time; in the long run, it is counter-productive. Coaches and professors who rely on fear to motivate you might see you do what you are supposed to do, but this motivation to perform will disappear as soon as the threat disappears.

Intrinsic motivation is the better source of motivation; it is longer-lived and much more powerful because it is an internally generated desire to do something.

Of course, a study hall, or a classroom, or a gym needs to have a sense of order and purpose, or nothing is accomplished. If that discipline is accomplished through punishment, the sense of order is present, but the productive result is missing. This is why the most effective teachers, coaches, and study hall supervisors work to establish a culture of learning, a culture which encourages intrinsic motivation. Discipline is a function of intrinsic motivation and is simply defined as doing what needs to be done when it has to be done.

Motivation is purpose and passion; it is what enables performance. Great performances are NOT motivated by external factors; instead, great performances are motivated by internal factors. But it is not what motivates you to start the performance that matters, it is what motivates you during your performance to keep going regardless of the score or grade. This internal energy determines the focus and quality of the performance.

When you are motivated by the outcome, the grade or score, you are doing something because you want the reward; you are playing to win, not because you like the game. Extrinsic motivation pushes your focus to the wrong place; when you focus on the grade or the score, you are not focused on the educational process or game and your performance suffers. When you are motivated solely by an outcome, you are relying on something external for motivation which you cannot control. If that is your sole motivation, you will inevitably experience a low grade or losing score, which will cause you to lose motivation. And without motivation, you cannot perform at all.

What do I look for in a student (or player)? I like someone who wants to learn, who is always trying to get better, who is coachable, who continues to try and work hard even in the face of adversity, who wants to be here.

Attitude is a choice. Therefore, you simply choose to be here now, to embrace the process, to organize yourself to achieve daily goals and objectives, to do what needs to be done when it needs to be done. Since many of these daily activities are repetitive, it is prudent to establish a routine to help you be more efficient with your time and effective with the effort.

Commit to a routine to improve performance

Recently I met a former student on my way to the library. Since I had not seen him for several years, we spent a few minutes catching up. He had heard that I had retired from teaching and was doing something different. I took the opportunity to explain the academic support gig I had, and the academic weight room project embedded in that job.

After a brief synopsis of what I was doing and how I thought academic skills could be taught to enhance a student's confidence and competence, he shared with me. He told me that my emphasis on 'skills' in the classes he took from me were at least as important as the content or knowledge in any subject. Specifically, he thought it was the idea of a study routine that helped him be successful at university, perhaps more than anything else. It took a couple of semesters to realize he needed to put the system into play, but once he established a routine for preparation and recall for each of his classes, he became 'smarter' and the courses became easier.

During my 25-year career as a high school head basketball coach, I had my players start every practice with the same routine; this simple routine helped to further embed crucial, previously taught, athletic skills, techniques, and systems. As a classroom teacher, we had a similar routine for the start of class daily: a short formative assessment, or quiz, over previously covered material. And as part of the Academic Weight Room project at CSUB, I shared the strategy for a routine to improve content knowledge with students: what to do before, during, and after class.

A routine is something you do to enhance performance in school by engaging in a system, or a program, of activities that you do regularly and repeatedly which makes you more efficient in your actions, and through which you become better. Adams says the routines improve efficiencies and effectiveness and "help us to be happier because they reduce the stress of repeated, daily decisions."

According to Harry Wong in his book *First Days of School*, routines become a part of the student's rhythm, part of the daily experience, and help to remove distraction, enabling productive behavior, personal achievement, and movement towards goals and objectives. When your routine dictates you spend an hour doing your flashcard self quiz, you will just work through the flashcards as if it is a normal part of your day, because it becomes one.

To implement a routine, you or your coach decides what it is you need to do and you write it down in your calendar, in your agenda, or on the bathroom mirror, and do it every day. The key to this is that it is written down and you just commit to a consistent effort; you must do this regularly, and frequently, with the same attention to purpose each time.

The next chapter, the first that focuses specifically on the academic skill infrastructure, introduces the specific study routines BC/DC/AC. These skills help you to know what to do before class, during class, and after class, and how to execute the routine. Doing these three routines alone will save you time in your study and revision endeavors and your results will show almost immediate improvement.

Okay, huddle up. AMPS on three. One, Two, Three...

Chapter 6
Intro to BC DC AC

Background Story

During my first term as athletics academic support coach at CSUB, two female athletes in a 300 level biology class requested a meeting with me.

At our meeting, they asked if I knew anything about anatomy and physiology and, if not, could they have a tutor for this relatively difficult required course for all PEAK (Physical Education And Kinesiology) majors.

In the course of our initial conversation, I tried to get a picture of what they were doing before, during and after class. Very quickly, I concluded that their anxiety about poor performance in the class was not necessarily a function of their knowledge about anatomy (which could therefore be improved by a tutor) but rather a deficiency in their academic skill set.

Before getting them a tutor, I asked them to try something new. I gave them BC, DC, AC routines (which I detail in the next three chapters) and asked them to do everything suggested in each of the routine subsets for the next week or so, and then to check back in with a report. I told them that if they tried this routine / study skills, and things still looked bleak, I would get them a tutor. When they came back a week later, they were astounded by their progress. They realized the purpose of the class was to give them an opportunity to learn, not to weed out those who did not already know about anatomy.

This conversation was an example of one of many brief academic interventions I conducted during the term. During these sessions, I was able to help students embrace process rather than focus on answers/results. And these brief interventions grew into Academic Weight Room sessions I presented to larger groups and teams in an effort to proactively reduce our dependency on tutors. The next three chapters detail that study process, providing specific skills and techniques which enable the student to establish effective and efficient routines in order to improve content knowledge, retention, and recall.

This set of BC/DC/AC study skill routines is not the only way to study. If you check out YouTube, you will find hundreds of suggestions. What I have done is to distill the options into a set of skills and activities I consider to be best practices, similar to the way a coach distills all of the offensive and defensive options available to the team into a cogent philosophy and strategy that is easy to understand, teach, and execute.

The BC routine is like a 'scout' for your upcoming assignment/lecture. The text for this unit details how to effectively and efficiently prepare for class so you have some idea what the professor is talking about. Your pre-class scout includes a quick check of blackboard and syllabus, downloading the PowerPoint and quickly looking over it, creating the flashcards for terms, concepts, and symbols for that chapter and lecture, doing a quick read of the chapter to get an idea of what the professor is going to talk about and reading the chapter through, in one sitting, from beginning to end, if time allows.

The DC is the in-class routine that you will want to assimilate into your classroom experience every day. The text for this unit details what it means to be an engaged participant in class, including how to be a better listener, how to effectively and efficiently take notes, and how to best utilize those notes after class.

The AC is the after class routine you will want to assimilate. The chapter for this strategy provides a clear plan of action for an active, engaged learner, including specific strategies and tactics, to ensure the learning of the material just covered in class including a 10-minute note review right after class, next day, and end of week. It also includes an all-important flashcards routine, as well as a strategy for post-lecture reading for content comprehension.

Let's get started.

Chapter 7
BC: The Before Class
Study Routine

To become smarter, do this pre-class scouting report

Just as a coach prepares his/her players for the upcoming training session or game, the player must also prepare for the upcoming training session or game.

And just as the teacher prepares his/her lecture and classroom activities, the student must be prepared to participate and engage in that classroom lesson, lecture, or activity. It really helps you to have some idea about the topic and key concepts of the upcoming lesson *before* you walk into the classroom.

The professor said to "read the chapter"

A common instruction from the professor for the upcoming lesson is to 'read the chapter.' During a team-only study hall session, I usually had less than 20 students in the building and I normally asked each student what his/her plan for the study session was, so I had some idea of their needs for the time. (Eventually, we went to a written goals and objectives form for students who needed more help.)

When I asked one student about his plan for the evening, he told me the professor said he had to read the chapter in the textbook. That's an admirable goal, but counterproductive. In fact, many students intending to read an entire 20+ page chapter BEFORE knowing anything about the topic find themselves asleep after a few minutes. When I told him NOT to read the chapter and do a quick read instead, he looked at me like I was nuts.

About a week into the term, I asked another student during our regularly scheduled appointment if I could see his notes from the last class session he attended. He handed me a notebook for that class; the pages were mostly blank. When I asked him about this, he responded that he really did not know what to write down. He had tried to write everything, but couldn't, so stopped trying. Then he tried to listen for the important stuff, as he had been told by a previous advisor, but had no idea what was important. So he just sat there. If you don't have some idea of what the professor is going to be talking about, you will then sit in class listening with no idea as to what is important and what is not important. In that unprepared state, you will either take no notes, or you will try to write down EVERYTHING the professor says; either way you are ineffective and inefficient. A pre-class routine significantly reduces the pressure regarding what is (or is not) important.

The hour you spend on the before-class routine detailed in this chapter will better serve your needs than either effort by the students I have mentioned above. The routine prepares you for the upcoming classroom session; it enables you to use your time more efficiently, it prepares you for the lecture or classroom discussion, and it serves to help you begin to retain content knowledge.

The BC routine and how you implement it

As the course progresses, you will look to spend about an hour of preparation time, per class, a day or so before that particular class. So, if you have two classes on Monday, you must spend two hours on Sunday preparing for the classes on Monday. If you have one class on Tuesday, you have to spend one hour preparing on Monday for the classes on Tuesday. The four steps of the before class routine are detailed in the following paragraphs and need to be executed in the same order every day.

BC 1. An organized student is an efficient student

At the beginning of every study session, check the professor's blackboard or web page for new information, assignments, and notes or PowerPoints for the upcoming lecture. This should take no longer than 5 minutes.

Utilize an agenda, calendar, or time-tracker and check it every morning when you first awake. Spending a couple of minutes to create the preparatory set for the day as part of your BC routine will reduce your level of anxiety.

The course syllabus is important, so at the beginning of the term you should find it, print it out, and send a pdf copy to your academic coach.

Instructors utilize Blackboard, or a similar online classroom resource, to provide discussion boards, post lecture notes, PowerPoints of upcoming lectures, assignments, documents, resources and to post quizzes and links to online quizzes.

As soon as possible after the first meeting of the class, it is crucial to log on to Blackboard and click on EVERY link the instructor has provided. Quickly look over what you find, making a mental note about the contents so you have some idea what is there; click on any links or embedded documents. Then go to the next link or folder. Repeat this process until you have clicked on everything the professor has uploaded to his/her course blackboard.

By doing this, you have an idea what is there, what is expected, and where things are once you need to complete an assignment. Professors can see who logs on, when he/she logs on, and how often each student logs on – so be a student and use the information provided. Many Blackboard course pages are difficult to figure out, so it is imperative that you start to figure out right away how the professor has his/her page organized. What is easy and intuitive for the professor is not necessarily easy and intuitive for you.

BC 2. Have some idea about the upcoming lecture

Download the professor's PowerPoint for the upcoming lecture. Print out or create for your tablet a pdf version or handouts version of the PowerPoint with at least three slides per page; ask if you need help doing this. This should take no more than about 10 minutes.

BC 3. Create flashcards

Spend about 20 minutes actively looking for and writing down the key terms and definitions found in the text, as well as any additional terms offered by the professor as bullet points in the PowerPoint.

Using both the text and the PowerPoint, write down the terms you will likely need to know on one side of a flash card and the definitions for the bulleted terms from the PowerPoint or the terms to know (usually in boldface in the text) but almost always in the end of the chapter, on the other side.

Because you are going to study all of your class flashcards at the same time (interleaving), it might be beneficial to color code with your highlighter (draw a colored line across the top of the card) cards by discipline; for example, green for math, blue for science, red for history, yellow for other. Put the page number from the text where you found the definition on the card.

BC 4. Do a quick read

The quick read is a crucial part of your scouting report and should take no more than 20 minutes. First, read the chapter summary, if there is one. Then go to the vocabulary and read aloud to yourself each word followed by the definition, using your finger to underline and follow along as you say it. Then go to the first paragraph and read it in its entirety. Then go to the second paragraph and read the first sentence and the last sentence; repeat this for each paragraph through the first section of the chapter. Read the entire last paragraph of the section. Then do the same thing for the next section, until you have completed all sections and all paragraphs.

During the quick read, you are simply trying to figure out the gist of the chapter or book. The gist is the big idea, the essence, or the big picture; you are trying to figure out what matters, what the author wants you to know: important ideas, key terms, and definitions. You are trying to locate these, see them, read them, but not yet memorize them. You are also using this time to formulate some questions about what you are reading to better help you learn the material. See Chapter 12 on questions for an idea of the questioning technique you could benefit from each time you read.

The Quick Read Strategies differ slightly depending on the type of text you are reading. For your textbook (and other nonfiction), *do not* begin to read the chapter with the intent of starting at the beginning and reading each word to the end. When you do this, and you know nothing or little about the topic, you will soon find yourself semiconscious and/or asleep, and the time spent to that point will have been wasted. Whatever you decide to do, trying to read the assigned chapters the week of the exam just doesn't work. Chapter 10 in this book, *How to do a Quick Read*, provides more detail on how to do this part of the routine.

Preparing for a laboratory class meeting

Successful performance in a laboratory class session requires answers to the questions Why, What, and How before you get to the lab.

Why. Doing your pre-class scout will enable you to understand the purpose of the lab. Read the assigned lab practical before you get to the lab; it is surprising how many students think all they need to do is to show up. This is a waste of your time and a waste of the professor's time as well.

What. When you do your 'scout', you will have a good idea of the procedures, and the process you will be required to follow. If, after this pre-read, you have any questions, you have time to figure out the answer or ask prior to beginning the lab. Make sure you have all necessary materials, proper clothing, and safety equipment before you leave for class. Be on time and expect to be paired with another student or be part of a larger group.

How. This is related to what you are going to do. You have an understanding of the purpose, or why, and you have an understanding of what you are going to do during the lab. The lab manual and professor's instructions, including the information you get during the briefing at the beginning of the lab, will help guide the steps you will take during the experiment or lab procedure.

Conclusion

It is important to have some idea of what the professor is going to talk about and what the chapter or assigned reading is about, getting

Chapter 7

you that much closer to an in-depth understanding of the concepts you need to know. But to put yourself in position for success, you must also know what to do during class and apply the routine described in Chapter 8 in order to be an engaged student. And unlike the students in the opening story of this chapter, by embracing this routine, your note taking will be both efficient and effective.

Chapter 8
DC: What You Need to be Doing During Class

To be smarter, be an engaged participant in your classes

In his book *What the Best College Teachers Do*, Ken Bain makes a significant point: Knowledge is constructed, not received. This means you cannot simply go to class and expect that you will 'get' the knowledge of the professor. As I wrote earlier, learning is a process and one of the most important parts of that process is what you do in the classroom. The professor cannot give you learning; instead learning is the outcome of the effort you put into the educational process.

While the best teachers strive to stimulate your construction of knowledge – rather than the simple transmission of information – in the end this construction is really up to you. Indeed, I have had more than one student complain that it seemed like they were having to learn through 'self-instruction.' To a certain extent, this statement of complaint is true; construction requires you to participate, to do what seems like more work than the teacher. And this is difficult because it is so hard to stay engaged in the lecture-style classroom.

The reason this is so hard is because your academic success, at least in part, starts with the seemingly simple skill of listening in the classroom. But this simple skill is easily sabotaged. While you are listening to the teacher/professor, you are trying to take notes. Most students can write their notes with a pen at around 10 to 15 words per minute. While there are some students who can use a keyboard without looking at the keys at 60+wpm, those who have to use two fingers to hunt and peck will see their keyboarding speed to be around 20 wpm. Either way, keyboarding your notes on a laptop is discouraged for two reasons. First, there is recent research that indicates that students who take their notes by hand have better retention of the information than those who use electronic devices. And secondly, having that device in front of you is way too distracting!

You have enough problems without distractions adding to your challenge. This is because while you are trying to take notes by hand, the teacher/professor is speaking at about 120 words per minute. So no matter what you try to do, you can't get it all down. Some students record the lectures for post-class listening; I just don't see how this saves time. And if you are not in attendance, the absence of visual information reduces the value of that recorded lecture; a video recording, however, would be very valuable for an absent student. But it is not only the gap between your note-taking speed and the professor's rate of speech that is a problem...

The biggest issue you face is that your brain is thinking at somewhere between 400 and 500 wpm. What is going on in that time-space continuum that is your 'listening?' That extra brainpower you have fools you into thinking you have time for side conversations, excursions into social media on your phone, planning for future activities, or simply trying to do your homework during class. These distractions waste your money, sabotage and obstruct YOUR OWN academic progress, and cause you to miss the point of the lecture. Worse, the professor might call on you at exactly the same time you let your brain wander off, on a tangent. It is impossible for you to know what is being said, let alone analyze or evaluate it, when you are not focused on the proceedings; and this focus takes effort and discipline.

So what does an engaged student look like?

The DC routine for a lecture class

1. Sit near the front. When you are closer, you are almost required to pay attention. Besides that, the professor will appreciate that you are interested enough to engage in her/his presentation. This will pay dividends when you actually reach out to the professor early in the course.

When I was a classroom teacher one of the things I did on day one was to start a discussion of why students chose to sit where they did. Although many supervisors suggested I needed a seating chart, I chose to allow students to sit where they desired until something happened that required an intervention. Once the students were seated, I asked them to write down their name and why they chose to sit there. Then I reviewed the returned sheets and randomly asked students to respond, generally starting with those at the back of the classroom. Common sense (and my own experience as a student) suggests that students nearer the front are more engaged than those at the back; research corroborates this. It is just too easy to disengage when you are at the back. And, fairly or not, professors often ask more questions of those at the back in an attempt to keep them involved.

2. Purposefully engage; pay attention. Sit upright with feet on the floor. Lean slightly forward in your seat. Hats off, hoods off, sunglasses off, headphones put away in your backpack, earbuds out, phone off and put in backpack, laptop closed and put in backpack unless the professor specifically requires you to be logged on.

Referring to the first day activity, above, we also talked about the idea of paying attention vs looking like you are paying attention. That's why I instituted a rule of no sunglasses, hats, or hoods for both my student athletes at CSUB and students in my own classrooms. And putting elbows on the table with hands underneath your chin – so that you are propped up looking all attentive – does not work; it is just too easy to nap. Likewise, the attentive stare with the occasional nod of the head in agreement is seen as a ploy which does not fool the teacher or professor often.

While you don't want to focus on peculiar mannerisms (for example, don't count how many 'ums' or how many steps they take back and forth in front of the room) by the teacher/professor, there are things which can help you focus your attention. Watch his/her eye movement, eyebrows, and facial expression – they help to convey subtle differences in meaning. Likewise, look for changes in voice intonation, inflection, and volume. Indeed, it is often the case that professors talk in an almost whisper for the really important stuff.

To focus your attention, it also helps, in any situation where you are hearing someone speak but most certainly in a class lecture, to ask these questions:

1. What is the professor trying to share with me?

2. What are at least three key takeaways from this lecture?

3. How can I best take advantage of this opportunity I have to be here today?

3. Once you are paying attention, you are able to actively listen. You have already completed your BC routine, so you should be able to go into the class ready to actively engage with the lecture, seminar topic, or lab.

The pre-class routine helps you to predict what the professor is going to do or talk about; since you have some idea what is going to be said, you are able to listen for those key terms, crucial concepts, and stories which help to explain the information. Every time the professor says something – engage that comment like a journalist!

*   Why?

*   Who?

*   What?

*   When?

*   Where?

*   How?

Pay attention to the stories that are used to connect the material with a real event in order to help you to create the connection for better memory.

Actively listening is a function of a good attitude. A poor listener wastes time by doing these things: Saying to her/himself 'this is boring;' judging the professor or teacher; forming an opinion about something the professor/teacher says and jumping into an adversarial position based on that opinion.

How do you know what is important? What do you listen for? The answer is found in your pre-class preparation. Additionally, the professor/teacher will usually tell you his/her goals and objectives for the unit, class, or lecture. And even if they don't, the PowerPoint is usually set up to offer the bullets of the key points. And if that is insufficient, the textbook gives you the road map. Compare your lecture notes with what the chapter says and extrapolate what seems to be important.

4. Take notes. Do not use your laptop, phone or tablet for note taking; you learn better if you have written your notes down on paper. While the smart phone is a great tool and seems to be gaining traction as an all-purpose alternative to a laptop, it simply does not make sense to try to take notes or write a paper with that technology.

Using your flashcards and the downloaded lecture PowerPoint, you will be able to follow the professor and use notes to add depth to what you have *already* done. You are trying to make sense of what the prof is saying, not write down everything said. To take your notes, there is a version of the Cornell method that I advocate.

Divide your page (left to right) into two parts: two thirds of the page and one third of the page, separated by a vertical line.

The left side is where you write your 'notes.' In this space, you summarize, in your own words, what seems to be important as determined by your pre-class preparation. In this space, you include the gist of any stories the professor tells to help explain a concept; teachers often tell stories and provide anecdotal connections which help you to better remember what is being said. You might not remember the concept, but often you can recall the story about the concept which then serves as a pathway in your brain to that concept, definition, or meaning. If you have done your pre-class flashcard preparation, you will not need to write down the terms and definitions in your notes; have your cards with you and make additional cards if new terms come up during class.

The right side is where you write the three to five key concepts or ideas the professor tried to get across to you in the lecture. It's like the summary section to what you wrote down in the lefthand 'notes' section. As you are taking your notes, wait until you have listened and recorded what the teacher is saying before you put your summary key words or terms into the one-third page section. You always summarize before going to a new page or new topic or new concept or new section.

The professor is usually finished with a topic, concept, section (or even the entire lecture) when he or she asks for questions. When this happens, circle any term or explanation you just didn't seem to get or understand. Pay attention when other students ask a question and make notes regarding the answer AND the question asked by the student.

It is important to understand that most teachers/professors are generally not happy if they have to answer the same question more than once, so it is wise to pay attention!

Often, questions from reading or the previous lecture will be answered in today's lecture. If you have a question after today's lecture, try to answer it yourself when you do the AC routine the next day. If you still have a question for the professor about today's lecture and were not able to figure it out yourself, ask it at the next lecture. Often the professor will start class with an offer to answer questions you might have from previous material or lectures. Chapter 13 of this book is devoted to questions.

5. Review notes. At the end of class, spend 10 minutes with your notes. Cover the notes part and look only at the key terms and concepts. As you read each key term/concept, re-create the professor's lecture; recite what he/she said regarding those terms. If you cannot re-create the lecture and define the key terms from those few words/terms, take a look at the notes.

Sometime the next day, spend another 10 minutes doing this review/recall process. Cover the notes, look at the terms and define them, talk about them, and try to reconstruct what the teacher said in the lecture.

You might do this again in about a week, although you will likely get better results for time spent through self quizzes with flashcards or end of chapter problems.

Conclusion

While showing up is crucial to success, simply showing up is not enough to make you a better student. Because academic success is a process, you will enhance your academic progress if you adopt the strategies and techniques for engagement in the classroom: listening, note taking, and note review.

The routine detailed in this chapter is difficult because of the distractions you must handle. However, when you engage in the recommended way, your comprehension improves because you are necessarily seeing and/or hearing the key concepts three or four times. Once you write down the terms, explanations, and related stories and review them right after class, again the next day, and again about a week later, you do not need to spend any more time with the notes. Indeed, as you will see in Chapter 9, which gives you details on your crucial after class study routine, DO NOT rewrite your notes; do not highlight or underline them. If anything, you can circle terms and ideas you are having trouble with so you can ask a question in class the next day.

Chapter 9
AC: The After Class
Study Routine

These study strategies will help you improve the most in the least amount of time.

Remembering 'what you need to know' is one of the most valuable techniques in this book. It puts your focus on the most productive techniques and strategies for academic success.

Unfortunately, one of my student athletes chose to try to embed knowledge by spending hours on her notes. She took copious notes in class, and then spent most of her study time re-writing her notes, using different colored ink, turning her serviceable notes into exquisite notes. I was never quite sure why she needed to write the notes more beautifully. In the end, this significant time killer did not result in better scores. As hard as I tried to convince her to adopt a different strategy, such as the one in this chapter, she simply thought her method was best: "I got it PapaCon."

The discrepancy between her grades and the extensive yet incredibly unproductive time spent on beautifully rewriting her notes was too much for her to overcome. Her strategy was eating up any time she had available to study and was not benefitting her at all. While some students (like her) put a reasonable amount of time and effort into strategies that research shows are unhelpful, others have learned from a teacher or parent or figured out by trial and error a better way to learn. They adopt at least some variation of this after class routine whilst others look for shortcuts.

There are No Shortcuts.

Rafe Esquith, an award-winning educator, titled his memoir *There are No Shortcuts*. It was written primarily for other educators, but his message resonates with parents and others who care about education. His stories told us that outstanding results are possible in spite of perceived detriment, poor funding, and under-privileged backgrounds; what is required is an organized classroom where students understand procedures, where they display a willingness to adhere to those protocols, a willingness to put time and effort into routines that enable higher achievement. Unfortunately, one popular shortcut involves academic malpractice, which I address in a later chapter.

That there are no shortcuts seems to be obvious but not widely accepted by most students. And because there are no shortcuts, to be a successful student requires diligent effort, hard work, persistence, organization, and strategies to enable you to better remember what it is you are supposed to know out of that class. Because most college level courses are currently offered as lecture courses, with some on-line hybrids, students necessarily have to engage, to actively participate in their own learning. The passive nature of the lecture, or the clickthrough to the right answer on some online courses, requires students to figure things out independently. What you do after the class or lesson will determine what you remember about that class or lesson and this routine is where the concept of hard work really comes in. Learning occurs when you consistently and regularly apply yourself to this routine.

The key to successful scores on any exam is knowledge or your comprehension of the content you are expected to master. When you answer an exam question, you must be able to recall the information to prove knowledge; this means you must be able to define the term, concept, or idea presented in the question, including a thorough description and/or explanation within the context of the question.

Then you have to connect that knowledge to an applicable formula, Venn diagram, graph, or concept (this is called application). Once you have done this, you will proceed through analysis where you make the connections, show cause and effect, explain what happens (happened) and how.

After a thorough analysis, you will want to go through the process of evaluation, which is to identify the pros and cons of the solution to the problem, clarify how each stakeholder is affected, and then weigh up where you think the evidence lies. In many cases, there is not necessarily a right answer that can be memorized; instead, the professor is looking for an understanding of the concept and evidence of your ability to think both critically and creatively as you identify the problem and arrive at a solution. Thus, your ability to arrive at an understanding of the material, the knowledge, is a process just as your ability to answer any given question is a process.

In the book *Make it Stick*, Brown et al say the most popular strategies for study include highlighting textbook and class notes, underlining text material and class notes, reading over notes repeatedly, and re-reading the textbook material. They go on to say that these widely used strategies are generally NOT effective.

Instead, they want you to ask yourself these questions:

- Have you used the key concepts in the back of the chapter to test yourself?

- Can you use a key concept in a paragraph?

- Can you quickly and easily define a key concept or term?

- Have you paraphrased the key idea in a lecture or paragraph in your own words?

- Have you tried to relate key ideas to something you already know?

- Have you found or connected the concept with outside examples or stories?

There are two keys to the retention of material you need to know. Medina in *Brain Rules* says 'remember to repeat, repeat to remember.'

Brown, meanwhile, says the key to making your learning stick is the concept of interleaving, which means you study all of your courses simultaneously. It is better for you to group subjects rather than study them one at a time. This grouped study, or interleaving, builds a more robust myelin wrap. The more you engage that neurotransmitter pathway, the more dense the myelin becomes, and the more expert you are in that skill or knowledge. Indeed, Colvin says, "You build your skills, your knowledge, by wrapping the myelin in those neurotransmitter pathways using deliberate practice." In this case, deliberate practice is simply engaging in repeated self-quizzing in an organized and specific manner, specifically adopting Brown's strategies of interleaving and spacing. Embedding knowledge is similar to the way athletes build strength in the weight room: intellectual and academic strengths decay in the same way that physical strengths decay and both go away if they are not maintained, and used, via repetition over time.

AC: The After Class Routine

Your after class routine should take about an hour, in 10- to 20-minute chunks. While you will spend 10 minutes on your notes right after class, the bulk of your after class routine is done the next day, but some activities will occur regularly during the week and term. Whenever you study, put your phone in airplane mode and move it away from you. Respond to calls, texts, or notifications only during one of your 5-minute breaks after 20 minutes of study.

AC 1. Notes review

As soon as possible after class, spend 10 minutes on the material just covered. Quickly go over the key concepts from your notes. Cover the left two thirds of your notes with a piece of paper and using only the right one third, try to recreate the lecture and define the key terms by looking at the key ideas and terms you have written down to summarize what you wrote in the left two thirds of the page. Try to remember as many things the professor said as you can, using only the few words you wrote on the right side. The first review of your notes will occur immediately after class.

Then sometime in the next day or two, spend another 10 minutes doing another note review from the most recent lecture in that class. This will be the second time you have covered the notes, trying to recreate the lecture and explaining the terms that are left showing; you are doing the same thing you did right after class. If you desire, you can do this 10 minute notes review one more time about a week later, but before the quiz. This three-step notes review for each class session enables you to spend at least 20 minutes (and up to 30 minutes) reviewing the key concepts from your notes.

AC2. Self-quiz: repeat to remember

In addition to the above notes review you will do at least every other day, space your study out over the rest of the quarter by spending about 20 minutes every day with your flash cards. Quiz yourself every day with the flashcards you created during your BC/Before Class routine which include the key concepts and terms in the lecture/chapter.

- Box/deck 1 is the set of cards called 'Don't Know It' and is covered every day.

- Box/deck 2 is the set called 'Know It' and is utilized every three days.

- Once a week, you challenge yourself with cards from box/deck 3, also called the 'Got It' set of cards.

The boxes/decks will see an increase in flash cards with every class you attend. By the end of the term, most words and concepts should be in your third box/deck. To better understand how to create and use flashcards, see the chapter on Flashcards.

In addition, you must go to the end of the chapter and spend another 20 minutes answering at least three randomly selected questions before going on to define the terms listed in the same chapter review. Doing this is a form of self-quizzing, but most students do not regularly work the problems and answer the questions. Instead, the norm seems to be to let any sort of content recall happen during the cram sessions right before the exam. Brown says that cramming is simply a form of binge and purge which does not lead to retention nor any form of meaningful learning.

A nice addition to flashcards is to utilize @quizlet, which is an app for your phone or tablet that lets you set up self-quizzes and access self-quizzes others have created for similar courses.

Putting old tests or pretests to work

One of the best things your professor can do for you is to give a pre-test at the beginning of the course; this gives you an idea what you know, what you don't know, and what you need to do to gain the knowledge the professor thinks you need to have.

Another tool that your professor could use which will highly benefit you is what I used to call clicker quizzes. As an instructor fortunate enough to have a smart-board in my classroom (with accompanying remotes for each student) I was able to give a quick 10-point quiz every day; I recorded the score and gave the student a chance to get half the missed points back when the correct answer (along with an appropriate source) was submitted by the next day. Unfortunately, students have learned to hate exams of any type. Still, I am convinced formative exams like this are among the most powerful ways to enhance the acquisition of content and knowledge.

Fortunately, you can quiz yourself, even if your professor does not. A key point in Brown's book is that regular self-quizzes (i.e. regular retrieval practice) have a significant impact on learning. In the few days before your exam, look over the comments from your professor on your past papers, and quiz yourself from your flashcards.

AC 3. Read

The final part of your After Class routine is to read the chapter in one sitting; according to Brown, it does not help to do this more than once. To focus your attention, read with a purpose; when reading the chapter or selection is to answer this question: What is the author saying?

To best figure that out, read the chapter or assigned reading through in one sitting from start to finish; if you encounter a term you still don't understand or have questions, circle it and keep going. Read in 20-minute segments; after 20 minutes take a 5-minute break to check your phone, get something to eat, use the facilities. Then read for another 20 minutes, with a 5-minute break; keep going until you finish. For some, it will take you 20 minutes to read the chapter; for others, it might take an hour or more. Since you have done the BC routine, including the quick read, the material by now should start to make some sense.

To read with efficiency and to achieve your purpose, find a quiet location with minimal distraction. While there is conflicting research regarding a person's ability to concentrate, as your academic coach I think it is necessary to turn off your phone or put it on silent and move it to a different room. Music in the background is okay as long as the music is ambient and quiet in nature without a lot of change in rhythm or beat; not much music is like this.

According to most research, rock, country, hip-hop, etc., do not work, regardless of what you think, mostly because of the lyrics but also to a lesser extent the heavier beat. In turn, trying to read with conversations or talk radio or television in the background is detrimental.

Conclusion

The After Class routine enhances your knowledge by developing and improving the skills of retention, recall, and comprehension. The technique Brown calls 'spacing' enables you to regularly refresh the information and strengthen your learning. With any learning, the amount you retain drops off with time, but when you come back to it daily, you regain that original level of retention. And as a bonus, when you make this daily routine a part of your life, you will find preparing for exams 'no big deal.' Who knows, it is very possible you will even find yourself with some free time the night before the exam.

Chapter 10
How to do a Quick Read

In Chapter 7, I told you to improve your efficiency while preparing for a class by doing a quick read instead of trying to read the chapter from beginning to end. This chapter tells you how to do that.

This chapter enhances your academic infrastructure by explaining exactly how to execute a quick read, which is an integral part of the before-class routine presented in Chapter 7. Once you have done a preliminary read of the assigned chapter(s) you will be able to take better notes, and you will be able to read the chapter(s) with better understanding after class. There is simply no reason to try to read the entire chapter before you go to class. Instead, do these steps.

First, go to the end of the chapter and read the chapter summary, if there is one, for the assigned chapter(s) for that day's lecture.

Then read the chapter title, and read the section or paragraph titles of each section/paragraph in the chapter.

Then go back to the beginning of the chapter and **read aloud** to yourself (if possible, if you are alone and not bothering others) only the sentence(s) of each paragraph containing the important words highlighted in bold face, using your finger to guide yourself as you go through the chapter. Do not worry if you don't understand anything yet; just quickly move through the chapter without lingering or trying to figure out the overall meaning of stuff.

Then go back to the beginning of the chapter and **read aloud** to yourself the first paragraph of the chapter.

If the chapter has more than one section, read the first paragraph of each section. Then read only the first and last sentence of subsequent paragraphs of that section. Then read the entire last paragraph of the section. Repeat for the next section and proceed until finished with the chapter. If the chapter is not divided into sections, simply read the entire first paragraph, the first and last sentences of each subsequent paragraph, and the entire last paragraph.

As you quick-read each section or paragraph, you are trying to figure out what the lesson is about while you begin to familiarize yourself with the terminology.

The quick read strategy for fiction is slightly different

Before starting to read an assigned book of fiction, do an overview, or cursory reading, of the book: read the front and back cover/jacket, to get an idea about the book and the author; read the Table of Contents, or read the chapter titles (if there is no Table of Contents); check to see if there is a discussion guide or set of questions at the end of the book; quickly look them over.

From class discussion, the syllabus, or the assignment the professor has given, you are trying to figure out *why* you are reading the book, including the expectations the professor has for you and what you are expected to learn from reading the book. Generally, there is more to the assignment than the story/plot itself and you are looking for the connections, the meanings, and the lessons.

Before reading, do some general research about the book, the topic, and the author; this is NOT an alternative to actually reading the book so don't look at this step as a shortcut. See if there is a Wikipedia entry about the topic or title and Google the book or author to find reviews and comments which will give you some idea. For example, last year at CSUB the students in the first year English courses were all assigned to read *The Immortal Life of Henrietta Lacks* by Rebecca Sloot. I am not sure exactly what the professors expected of the students regarding this book, but it would surely have helped if each student was aware of the general nature of the topic (cell research) and the ethics of doing research on cancer cells without the patient's knowledge or permission.

Once background information has been gathered, begin the quick read, which should take about 20 minutes. Again, as with non-fiction textbooks, you should do a quick overview before reading from beginning to end. First, scan through for characters; make a list of who/name, what they seem to be doing, where they are. Read the first paragraph, then read the last paragraph of the chapter or chapters you have been assigned. Go back to the beginning of the chapter and skim through relatively quickly; circle or write down any terms you don't know or understand. In the margin, write a two or three word summary of that paragraph; this is the gist, what the author seems to be saying, or the big idea of that paragraph. Through this, you are beginning to chunk information into easier to remember bits summarized into your own words.

Conclusion

This chapter provided the details about a quick read. Moving on, Chapter 11 does the same for perhaps the most crucial component of your before-class study skills routine: how to create and utilize flashcards.

Chapter 11
How to Create and
Utilize Flashcards

Utilizing flash cards will do more to enhance your academic infrastructure, improve your knowledge, and prepare you for an exam than any other strategy.

Recently I had the opportunity to chat with a former student about what I was doing now that I had retired. I told him about the Academic Weight Room project and as we discussed what the project includes, I touched upon how valuable flashcards are in the learning process. He interrupted, "Oh flashcards are a necessity when you are sitting for the series seven exam." He went on to explain how important this strategy was in his own post-university advancement in investment banking. Indeed, almost every professional career requires some sort of examination which demands complete understanding of terminology and concepts. Flashcards are the most efficient way to embed such knowledge and ace any exam.

How to Create and Use a set of FlashCards

As Medina says, repeat to remember. And as Brown says, space your study out and study all classes simultaneously. Self quizzing (during every day of term time) using the Leitner flashcard system recommended by Brown is the most efficient and effective way to meet this objective.

To put this system into practice, get three 3x5 card boxes and a bunch of 3x5 file cards; you can also use jumbo clips instead of boxes to hold together each deck/box of cards. My version of flashcard utilization is a variation of the system Brown recommends in his book. Students who already use flashcards generally have a separate set of cards for each class, but Brown's research says to put all cards for all classes into one deck.

The key to doing well in any discipline is to know and understand the language of that discipline, which is simply a function of the terminology. As you memorize and assimilate that terminology, or language, into your daily life, your understanding grows. And according to both Medina and Brown, the best way to accomplish this assimilation is through the use of flashcards.

As I wrote in Chapter 7, the before-class routine for each class requires you to create a flash card for each important concept or term covered in the text or lecture. Again, you use both the professor's PowerPoint and your textbook as the source of any terminology you need to know. Of course, the term goes on one side and the definition goes on the other and is done as part of the BC/Before Class routine. And remember to put the page number or source of the definition on the card. All cards from all classes go together; **don't** separate them to study each class independently.

You could also create flashcards for ANY information you need to remember and which you will be tested on; for example, if you are having trouble with terminology from practice – such as offensive or defensive plays/calls – create cards for those plays, terms, signals, or calls. And, as I have said previously, it might help to color code the top of the card according to your class in case you want to pull out all the cards for one class for a quick review right before an exam.

Box/Deck 1: Don't Know It

Into box/deck 1, put all the cards you have created for that day's class/lecture and any other activities for which you need to be able to recall information. The next day, after class, go through the cards by yourself or with a teammate, roommate, friend, academic coach, or tutor. If you know the correct answer/definition immediately, put that card into box/deck 2, which contains the information you seem to know after a couple of days. If you make a mistake or simply cannot recall the answer, leave the card in box/deck 1. You should go through box/deck 1 every day, as you are constantly adding new material/cards from classes you attend every day. Going through this don't know box/deck can be done in 10 to 20 minute intervals during the day or at your dedicated after class study location, as long as you get through the complete deck once every day.

Box/Deck 2. Know It

You should go through box 2 every three days or so, say every Wednesday and Saturday. If you cannot recall the correct answer when you quiz yourself out of box/deck 2, move the card to box/deck 1, but if you recall the information correctly, move the card to box/deck 3.

Box/Deck 3. Got It

You quiz yourself from the cards in box/deck 3 once a week, say every Sunday night. If you cannot recall something that is in box/deck 3, you must move it all the way back to box/deck 1 so you can get more coverage. However, if you know the information on the card in box/deck 3, leave it until next week. Your goal is to have everything you need to know moved into box/deck 3 by the final exam.

Conclusion

This chapter provided you with a detailed explanation of how to create and use flashcards. This one component of your academic skills infrastructure might do more than anything else to improve your knowledge and performance and is perhaps the most important part of the three study skills routines previously discussed. In earlier chapters, I introduced the idea of the flashcard but reserved the details until now, simply because this skill set is so crucial.

The next chapter changes pace slightly as I talk about the importance of questions. While a teacher or professor might use a shared inquiry or Socratic Seminar approach (which is arguably the most beneficial for students) it is also likely to be the one with which students are least familiar. I think this is because it is the most difficult to put into practice for most teachers in most schools, perhaps due to the simple constraints of large class sizes.

It is my intention to help you to understand how to question by first explaining in detail how the teacher in the shared inquiry classroom organizes the topic around questions and enhances your learning by forcing you to think about both the question and the answers provided by everyone in the class. In the end, this will help you to become a better questioner, improving your critical thinking skills!

Chapter 12
On Questions

"In our classrooms, it shouldn't be just about the acquisition of knowledge, but what we may do with knowledge in the face of a question." Jeff Goldstein.

Your coursework is not just about acquiring knowledge about a particular subject. While knowledge is the first step in the process, you are striving to gain understanding and comprehension which you then apply as a solution to a problem or as an answer to a question on an exam. As a VCB colleague has said, the educational process moves from acquisition of knowledge to the application of knowledge.

Questions are the best way to get beyond the simple acquisition of knowledge to understanding, comprehension and application. Some teachers use questions in an effort to push you toward the acquisition of understanding, but the most powerful approach a teacher utilizes is to move beyond a teacher-centered classroom to a student-centered discussion where the students ask the essential questions and the teacher simply guides the discussion.

Understanding the nature of questioning by the teacher will help you to be better prepared to answer questions, but more importantly, it will help you to be become better at asking questions and questions help you to become smarter. To that end, this chapter uses the teacher's perspective to help you develop better questioning skills.

I am not sure who said this, but it resonates: Smart students don't have all the answers; smart students strive for comprehension through questions. Asking questions helps you to learn. In business, questions help everyone get to solutions. It is important to adopt the mindset that questions help you through the educational process rather than being some sort of sign of deficiency. Over the years, I found that most students did not really want to ask questions during class; maybe it was because they thought they would look less smart than the others. I am pretty sure that if they had questions they were afraid to ask, others did too. Those in the room who seem smarter don't have all the answers but often they are the students who ask questions. Questioning helps you learn. Questions in the classroom, whether by the teacher or other students, help everyone to better understand the concepts.

The Nature of Questioning

It is likely that you will find yourself in a small-enrollment seminar class, which utilizes a shared inquiry approach, at some point in your coursework for your major. It is more likely for those in humanities and social sciences than for math and science majors, but the advantages of a shared inquiry class are significant, so the professor might spend at least some time with this approach. Understanding the nature of questioning, which is the essence of the shared inquiry classroom, will help you to be better prepared to answer questions, but more importantly, it will help you to be become better at asking questions.

A professor/teacher who uses a question-centered shared inquiry approach will talk very little and instead serve more like a traffic control officer, enforcing protocols and rules to keep the classroom in order, arguments in check, and most students engaged. This is often a challenge for students who have experienced only a lecture-based classroom.

Because teachers in this model only ask questions, and do not necessarily answer questions from students, participation in the learning process by everyone in the room is a prerequisite. This seems to run contrary to the (mistaken) perception that students attend class to 'get information' or to absorb the professor's knowledge and information. When you take a course from a professor who utilizes the shared inquiry model, you simply will not be able to sit back in a passive way even if that is the way you have engaged other classes.

The key to a successful experience in a class utilizing this type of approach is to engage in the classroom and to diligently prepare prior to stepping into the room (see BC/Before Class Routine). The assigned text serves as the focus of the discussion and any questions, and necessarily the answers must come from that text. This makes it impossible for you to engage unless you have read the text; in fact, in many shared inquiry classrooms, only those who have read the text and are able to cite specific passages in their own answers can even participate. While this sounds fine, it really is not a good situation in which to find yourself; if your assessment is a function of participation, you will be on the lower end of the assessment metric.

To embrace the process, you must prepare and you must understand the types of questions you will be asked as well as the kinds of questions that will best serve your needs.

Types of Questions

Every teacher asks at least some questions, for a variety of reasons. In fact, research reported in 1991 by William Wiley in *Questioning Skills for Teachers* said the average high school teacher asks about 300 questions per week or about 10 per classroom period. Research and information about questioning skills is almost entirely devoted to the teacher rather than the student. So, I am going to share with you what teachers are trying to accomplish, and how they ask questions, as a way to help you become a better questioner in your own classes. According to Wiley, the most common and most familiar to all students is the question designed to determine your basic understanding of the facts, terminology, or definitions in order to confirm that you, and perhaps all of the other students, are 'getting it' before moving on. A factual question has a correct answer, which is usually relatively easy to find and memorize. This answer is a function of your BC study routine during which you did your required reading.

According to Bill Cathers, who provides consulting services for teachers who want to utilize the shared inquiry approach, teachers will ask interpretive questions for which there is sometimes more than one appropriate or possibly correct answer. For this type of question, you will be required to provide support for your answer with information, quotes, or words from the text; you cannot simply provide a vague answer with a strong assertion of opinion nor can you use any sort of personal experience or current events information to support your position. When providing an answer to an evaluative or interpretive question, you will be expected to support your opinion with evidence from the text being discussed. Cathers says this type of questioning (which asks you to demonstrate comprehension) is the most difficult questioning you will hear in a shared inquiry classroom. A question which requires not only factual information from the text, but also interpretation, analysis and evaluation (see Chapter 14 for further discussion) will force you to arrive at an answer by utilizing higher level thinking skills; this process strengthens your academic skills, which makes you smarter. One reason why so many K-12 and Year 1- Year 6 classrooms are moving to the shared inquiry approach is because everyone in the classroom becomes smarter, both individually and collectively.

The shared inquiry approach is designed to move the student into a higher level of critical thinking, resulting in a better understanding of the concepts. Teachers also use questions to stimulate student participation in class, to review previously studied material, to personalize the subject in order to make it more relevant to the student, and to control behavior. Wiley constructed a Venn diagram in his document for teacher use in which he visualizes questioning in three circles: circle 1 is the subject of discussion, circle 2 is the personal reality of the student, and circle 3 is the external reality. A good question from the teacher encompasses all three components. It seems to me that if a student can also construct his/her own questions in this same model, it would help deliver a better understanding of the material.

It is my belief that the more types of questions a student is exposed to in any context or confronted with in the classroom, the better he/she will understand how to ask a question. But what if the student's teacher is not adept at questioning, resulting in exposure to only the easiest and most fundamental lower-level question type in the Bloom Taxonomy?

The answer lies in this discussion of questioning and my attempt to provide the student with the same type of questioning strategies that teachers have had access to for years; perhaps by better understanding the teacher's perspective, the student can assimilate some of those same skills.

Teachers generally construct questions with Bloom's Taxonomy in mind. Low-level questions would be those which query content knowledge and comprehension and require simple memorization as well as skills of observation by the student. Questions in this lower order category test recall and recognition.

The next level of question in Bloom's Taxonomy would be questions to query the student's ability to apply terminology or a formula in order to arrive at a simple answer to a given problem, to demonstrate understanding, to compare and contrast, and to explain what something is.

Level three is analysis, and requires the student to demonstrate higher level critical thinking skills to determine why, possible motives, cause and effect relationships, and how something works.

The fourth and top level requires students to demonstrate skills in synthesis and evaluation. Questions at this level, such as 'determine the extent to which', require the student to evaluate, create possible solutions, and predict outcomes. This type of question is common in most high school and college exams, but less common in many classrooms. With that basic understanding of where the teacher is coming from, it is easier to construct a model for your use.

In order for you to be able to ask any question at all, you must have a basic understanding of the vocabulary, terminology or language of the course. What is first required is that you memorize the terms and definitions so you have a better understanding of what the teacher is actually saying in class. If you don't have that basic understanding of the vocabulary, many things become difficult to understand and even a question of clarification is unlikely to help. Once you are able to speak using the same vocabulary – a better question necessarily emerges.

Questions to Avoid

It is incumbent upon the professor/teacher to measure the student's understanding, which usually requires a question with something other than a yes/no answer, or even a short quiz. But that does not exclude you from asking for a better explanation of the words, terms, concept, or theory. That said, the most frustrating question from a student for a teacher is "I don't understand" because the professor has likely just spent an entire class, or more, explaining exactly that.

When you don't understand something after the teacher's explanation, you need to figure out a way to be more concise about what it is you don't understand. It is likely you can figure out the answer during the AC/after class routine, but if (after doing that) you still don't understand, you will at least have a more specific starting point. Because you can refer to the material you do know and have covered, including your notes and flashcards, you can reduce the breadth of your confusion or uncertainty, or lack of understanding, and instead focus on what is more likely a lack of depth. A question which proclaims a general, vague, lack of understanding is seen as lazy, and requires you to recognize that education involves your personal engagement.

A multi-part question is frustrating for the teacher because it is often too broad to elicit any sort of valid answer within the constraints of the lecture. In my classroom, I found that I simply forgot the second two parts after answering the first.

Another counter-productive question in the classroom is one that is a particular time-thief; that's a statement of opinion disguised as a question. Of course, this is not confined to academia (you see it on news reports all the time) but the prevalence of this type of question does not give you license to do the same in your class. This statement of opinion is a rude and blatant attempt by the 'questioner' to hijack the teacher's lecture or presentation in order to use the 'question' as a forum for their own position.

Where Your Questions Come From

During the lecture, write down and circle any term or explanation you just don't seem to get. The most common question you can ask is one for clarification of the material, which I pointed out earlier is at the lowest level of critical thinking. And that is okay; if you have done your after class study routine and something still doesn't make sense, by all means ask about it. Often, questions you might have from reading or the previous lecture will be answered in the next lecture, either through an unprompted clarification from the professor (sometimes simple repetition with a different analogy helps) or through a question from another student.

If, after you have unsuccessfully tried to answer your question yourself during your AC routine and you have not heard the answer after having listened carefully in the subsequent lecture, ask your question; often professors will start a class with an offer to answer questions you might have from previous material or lectures. The best way to ask a question to further your understanding is to ask the professor/teacher if you understand 'x' concept correctly which is then followed by your understanding. Doing this strengthens your own self-esteem when you have figured it out on your own, and if you didn't get it, helps to clarify without hurting your self-esteem since you did try to figure it out. Again, the process is the key thing, not necessarily the answer.

Pay attention in class when other students ask a question; the teacher/professor generally is not happy if he/she has to answer the same question more than once.

To enhance your understanding of the material, it helps if you ask yourself questions while reading. Whether you quick read the chapter or thoroughly read the chapter, you want to think about these questions:

- What is the key concept or idea?

- What does it mean?

- How does it relate to other ideas and terms and previous chapters?

- Why does the author think this is important?

- How does it work?

- Why does it matter?

Questions like these that engage the thinking skills of application, analysis, evaluation, or synthesis are the best questions you can ask. This approach serves to improve your own understanding and will help others in class as well because it enables the professor to initiate a class discussion.

Analysis usually starts with a simple *why*. It enables you to dig into a concept to figure out how it works, or how something is connected to something else, or what causes the particular outcome. When digging deeper through the use of *why* questions, you will necessarily have a basic understanding of the term or concept, including the definition. This enables you to understand what it means in the context of the discussion. But in addition to figuring why something is happening and how it works, you are trying to answer the question 'Why is that?' for each level. This questioning model might sound sort of redundant, but asking why something is happening at each level gets you to a deeper understanding of the concept.

This then enables you to see the cause and effect connections and figure out the pros and cons of the proposed actions. Analysis moves from how and why to the cause and effect connections to the evaluative questions and answers regarding who is affected, how they are affected, and why. These analytical and evaluative questions are often open-ended, and do not necessarily have a conclusive right or wrong answer. While this type of question from the teacher is designed to engage you and help improve your understanding, your usage would indicate growth in your own academic skill set.

Conclusion

Remember, questions help you learn. The professor/teacher is not the font of all knowledge, but rather the facilitator of your quest to become smarter: a partner in your educational process. It is the questions which make you smarter, not just the answers.

This chapter was included to make the process of questioning easier to understand and implement. The next chapter talks about preparing for an exam and how to handle the exam, including how to manage your time, how to break down an exam question, how to write an essay question answer (more easily) when you use an efficient structure, and how to utilize the command words in a question to drive your answer.

Chapter 13
Handling the Exam

"Why hasn't someone told us this before?"

Almost 100 students (all non-athletes) were in attendance for our most popular Academic Weight Room session. At the end of the presentation, a student responded to my offer to answer questions. He asked if he could stand, and I suggested he did not really need to, but said sure. He asked me, "Why hasn't someone told us this before? This is the most helpful lecture I have ever heard." In response to his comment, I said most professors/teachers either don't have the time or they just assume you know how to handle an exam. Everyone seems to take this skill for granted, but I have found that few students really understand how to do this. Besides the three study skills routines, this is probably the most valuable chapter in the book.

Most professors (teachers) settle on a style which is unique to their teaching. However, every exam is designed to assess *your* understanding of the material. Therefore, we can learn to break down just about any type of exam and figure out an answer if we recognize that it all comes back to content knowledge and application, analysis, and evaluation.

Discovering a need

In Chapter 3, I told the story of a student who could not answer a question which she had never seen before. From that point on, it became my mission to make sure the students knew to handle any question they had not seen before. With my Chapter 3 student, I do not recall exactly what the question was, but this is an example:

The Bank of England's (Central Bank for UK) Monetary Policy Committee will meet to discuss the economy and what action would be appropriate in response to this assessment. At this meeting they can do one of three things: a. raise interest rates; b. lower interest rates; c. leave interest rates where they are. What do you think they will do and why?

While content necessarily differs, there is a strong possibility that every exam question requiring a written answer in every course you take will require you to address one or more of the four common hierarchical components which help the teacher to measure your comprehension. These are skills you can learn and/or develop and I will provide details which explain how to assimilate and activate these crucial skills which enable you better handle exams.

Know how to answer any question

"Too often coaches give players answers to remember rather than problems to solve."

This quote was tweeted by CSUB women's soccer Coach Gary Curneen, and originated from Dan Micciche who suggested that the best soccer players must make plays and adjustments on the field without instructions from the coach. In fact, it is nearly impossible in most sports for the coach to choreograph each action for each player because no game situation is exactly like a previous situation. The coach teaches skills, techniques, and strategies which enable the player to handle any situation as it arises. The more skilled the player becomes, the easier it is to handle these situations. The same holds true for examinations in academia. It is not a sound strategy to rely on remembering answers given to you by the professor or teacher.

Understanding concepts and terminology is different from memorizing answers. You must understand, but trying to memorize answers is a time-consuming endeavor with little payoff. Unless you cheat, or unless you are truly lucky, it is very unlikely you will know – in advance – what questions are in the exam. The essence of handling an exam lies in your ability to break down any question, especially those you have not seen before. Breaking down a question you have never seen is a form of problem solving. A process orientation helps you to develop skills which will better prepare you for the exam.

How to handle the exam

Implicit in all academic success is how well you have learned your content; after all, exams are designed for you to demonstrate your content knowledge and your ability to apply that knowledge and inherent formulae, graphs, and diagrams in your answer.

Perhaps the most overlooked skill is how to manage the clock during the exam but the most valuable skill is your ability to break down a question. Almost all summative exams involve questions which require a written answer. For these, it is beneficial to know how to best structure your written answer, which is predicated on your ability to recognize and understand the differences between the five levels of probable command words embedded in the question.

Finally, some exams contain multiple-choice questions, so I have included strategies on how to best handle those types of questions.

Prepare: study efficiently and effectively to understand content

In preparation for the unit, midterm, or final exam(s), you have (hopefully) been efficiently and effectively preparing as you have gone along by following the after class routine which includes the almost daily flashcard review and end of chapter problems. This will enable you to have a thorough understanding of the vocabulary, terminology, graphs, formulae, and concepts which will be covered. This will save you from having to spend time 'cramming' the night before.

Your teachers, parents, professors and coaches give you advice and encouragement to study hard. While there is nothing wrong with this, keep in mind that one of the explicit purposes of this book is to get you to engage in the process, which enables you to be efficient with your time and effective with the results, removing any need to try to learn it all at the last minute. Attention, focus, and hard work are all necessary and important, but studying 'hard' the night before will not be enough if you have not studied all along.

Following this same line of thought, it does you NO GOOD to re-read the chapters as preparation for the unit exams. Instead, spend at least an hour, but no more than two hours, studying. The first part will be a run-through of your flashcards; by the time you sit the exam, any information you are responsible for should be in either box/deck 2 or box/deck 3. The second part of your exam prep, or study, would be to go to the end of each chapter covered on the exam and quickly and correctly answer at least three randomly chosen questions (that you have not answered before).

Do not use chemicals to stay awake; do not lose sleep to cram. Instead, according to Anabelle Berklund, a former student in my classroom and current professor at Colorado State University, you are far better off getting sufficient sleep than you are going into sleep deficit to cram. Of course, if you have engaged in the entire BC/DC/AC process, the review should be relatively quick and easy; knowing that you understand the content will remove most of the stress from the exam.

Prepare: do a pre-exam scouting report

Every professor has a different method or style in the classroom and generally offers an exam style which can be considered typical of that person. It is important to discover the professor's exam tendencies, including M/C, essay, problem to be worked and solved, data response, and sometimes an oral defense of answers. Often this is difficult before the first exam, but many professors do offer suggestions and even sample exams to prepare from. And, in some cases, old exams are available to peruse.

A pre-exam scouting report includes using your own previous exams to prepare for subsequent exams in that class. One of my pet peeves as a teacher was to watch some students quickly look at the grade for a thoroughly commented and well-marked exam and then toss it into the trash. When you get a test back, study it for tendencies as well as for what you don't know. If you forgot an answer, or never knew the answer, by all means make sure you learn it. Figure out what you did wrong to ensure you don't make the same mistakes twice. After seeing my own hard work go into the bin, I decided to make students embrace this step; I required students to figure out the correct answer for questions missed and gave points back on the exam (extra credit to some extent). Even if the professor does not give you the extra credit, it will help you understand the material better if you do this yourself after every exam.

Execute: know how to apply formulae, graphs, and concepts you learned

Knowledge of the concepts and terms covered in your course material is the most important thing. This is retention, which is learning which makes recall possible, and requires tactics which enable you to embed that knowledge into memory which is accessible at the time of your exam, and ideally, when you need to apply it during your career.

Also crucial is the ability to apply this knowledge, or information, to answer questions and solve problems presented in the exam. This involves comprehension, which is your ability to understand fully what the material is about, what the concept is and/or does, and how you can apply this knowledge to a question in an exam.

It is important to be able to memorize a term and its definition, but you must be able to take that one step further and demonstrate that you understand how something works. This is particularly important with respect to formulae you are expected to know, understand, and use in an operation. Indeed, you have to know what specific symbols mean, what happens when they are engaged with variables, how the formula 'works', what the formula is supposed to tell us, and what the answers are supposed to mean.

Execute: create a spending plan for the time available

As mentioned, this skill is perhaps the most overlooked part of taking an exam. The first thing you must do when you sit down for your exam is to figure out your time constraints and create a plan for how you are going to spend the time available for the exam as whole and for each question individually.

Obviously, the overall time allotted for the exam by the professor drives your entire process. While a rule of thumb says you generally have about a minute per mark or point per question, whether they are multiple choice or written answers, you must fit that within the greater constraints of the time block granted for the exam. Multiple-choice questions do not require any planning time but you will want to strategically address them in the one to two minutes allocated to each question.

For written answers, you will want to spend about 30% of the allotted time in planning, including the process of breaking down the question. That leaves you 70% of the allotted time to actually write the answer. For example, if the exam is two hours and you have an exam that is worth 100 points, you would spend no more than 30 minutes planning and breaking down questions. However, if the exam is three 25 point questions in ONE HOUR, you will have to adjust this model accordingly. In this case, you would have no more than 20 minutes to plan and have 12 minutes to write the answer for each question.

Remember to spend appropriate time on questions with minimal possible marks or points. For example, if the question is 2 points, spend only a couple of minutes; do not write more than a couple of sentences. To most efficiently utilize your time during an exam, it is crucial that you understand the exam command words (see Chapter 15) and recognize that lower level words do not require as much time and response as higher level words.

In order to formulate your best written answer, don't just start writing. Have an idea what the question is asking, how much time you should spend on it, what the concept is, and how you are going to attack the question. It is crucial that you don't spend any more time on a question than you have allotted. A common mistake for students is to spend way too much time on early questions and too little time on latter questions, resulting in rushed and incomplete answers to questions that often require the most thought. The planning process includes breaking down the question; an example is provided next.

Execute: understand the question's 'command words'

Every exam question contains a key command word to guide your answer. The professor assumes you understand what these words actually mean. Sometimes these words are misunderstood. For detailed information on the command words used in most examination questions, refer to Chapter 15.

Execute: break down the question

With your spending plan jotted down on a corner of the exam, you then begin to break down the first question. While a question which requires a written answer almost always demands that you break down the question, some multiple-choice questions don't necessarily require this skill. This section is written with the essay question in mind. For this type of question, many students just start writing an answer, thinking inspiration is just a few words away. And sometimes students mis-read the question or simply see the question they want to see rather than the one that is actually posited.

Instead, begin the process by asking yourself these questions:

- What is the question asking you?

- How many parts are there to the question?

- What are the obvious concepts to address and what are the relevant, but hidden, concepts which need to be addressed?

- What are the key terms to keep in mind?

First, you have to read the question carefully to figure out what the question is asking. Then you craft a plan for your answer similar to the examples I relate below.

Think back to the question posed for my Chapter 3 student. How would you break that question down? In fairness, you might not have knowledge of economic policy and therefore could not possibly answer that question. But if you were in my class, you would be expected to have that knowledge and here is how I broke the question down for the class.

First, we had to break down the question into digestible parts: *What is the concept this question addresses?* In this case, it would be macroeconomics focusing on one of the tools a government has at its disposal to expand or constrict the economy.

What are the specific components, or parts, of that general concept of monetary policy addressed in this question? Basically, the central bank has the authority and ability to take steps to raise interest rates to constrain an inflationary economic situation, or lower interest rates in order to stimulate/grow the economy. Then you would be expected to identify all of these concepts: macroeconomics, central bank, monetary policy, inflationary gap, recessionary gap; define each; then explain what causes an event such as an inflationary gap or a recessionary gap in an economy and how monetary policy works to address each.

Then you would be expected to analyze what would likely happen when the bank raises interest rates, what would likely happen when they lower interest rates, and what would likely happen if the bank leaves interest rates where they are. While doing this, you would explain what tools the central bank has at their disposal to effect the change, how each tool works, why, and what happens with each, what cause and effect relationships exist.

The final part of the question implies, but does not explicitly ask, that you evaluate the pros and cons of the choices the bank could make. It asks for you to explain the action they are likely to take and why, so you will be expected to spend several sentences identifying the pros and cons of each option followed by your own take which explains why the option you support is the best option of those available.

Execute: know how to write about what you know

At the minimum, you must understand and be able to explain the what, how, and why of the question. Each question will pose challenges for you as the professor attempts to determine the extent of your knowledge in a variety of ways. Many students try to 'get by' simply by writing down all that they know about a topic, even if some of the information is not applicable. For your examinations, it is important to know the material. But it is not enough to simply know the material. You also need to know how to apply content to a problem, how to formulate a position based on the knowledge you possess, how to solve the problem posed by the examiner in a case study or problem presented, how to link the concept of the question to course concepts and theory and often the current world situation, how to analyze data and how to evaluate your information and position in the context of the question. So, for every question, at the minimum, you need to address these three levels:

For the what, or content, component of the minimum requirements, you must be able to explain, in at least two sentences, what the concept is; define it and explain how it fits or its implication in the question. Most students spend their entire time here; the professor wants to know the what, but you must realize there is more to the question than this. So, once the content is identified, defined, and explained, you must demonstrate understanding of how it works or fits. This means you must write at least three sentences of factual background, some history, and perhaps an example to help bring some depth to the explanation of WHAT. Then you will need to write at least three sentences discussing WHY it matters, why it is important, and you identify the cause and effect connections.

Execute: use an effective structure to write your answer

Chapter 16 provides detailed instruction into an efficient and effective essay structure you can apply to almost any essay exam question, writing assignment, or research paper. Once you learn to apply this relatively simple structure, your writing process will be less cumbersome. So embed and apply the essay structure I provide and take the time to consider the following points about writing the answer to exam question.

You will have to compose your essay within the framework required by the command word used in the question. In answering most questions which require a written answer, you will need to make three arguments or points, and support those three points or arguments with content and knowledge from the course and data from the case/question. In my experience, two supported points are better than seven points or pieces of information that would work, but which are not supported or connected. Every time you write any answer, make the connection between what you know from the course and lectures, and what the question is asking. Link content together with connections to get a string of ideas, support, arguments, or reasons why.

When writing your answer, you have in mind that you will need to address content, application, analysis and evaluation. You begin this process by establishing a connection between content and context; this is application and is the ability to pick up the two or three key concepts in the case, problem, article, or question and use those concepts to develop the answer in the context of the question, case, article, or problem. For every question, you should be able to identify the concept(s) you are being asked to use, define, explain.

Then you must be able analyze the question in the context of the course material. The skill of analysis is covered in detail in Chapter 14. If you give an example to demonstrate a connection or to explain how something works, keep it in context. If in the course you have been talking about female impressionist artists, don't use peanut butter as an example.

Finally, you must demonstrate the ability to evaluate, or show logical reasoning which is also covered in detail in Chapter 14.

If you are able to only cover content and application, it will be hard for the teacher or professor to award a score for that question that is much above passing. Still, it is possible you could pass the exam if you are able to demonstrate an understanding of all the concepts covered in the course by demonstrating your ability to define and explain the terms in the question and use graphs, diagrams, and formulae you learned in class to begin to arrive at an answer.

Execute: how to handle multiple choice questions

Multiple Choice (M/C) questions can be very, very difficult. Indeed, I often provided students with the opportunity to answer True/False questions with a third option of Not Sure, which required an explanation as to why. Of course, some students chose that because they were not sure and hoped that being solely not sure was an okay response. And in all cases where we utilized M/C or T/F, I allowed half credit for each question marked wrong that was corrected with the proper page number or source for the correct answer.

Sometimes with M/C exam questions, you will get a set of answers where ALL are somewhat or partially correct and you have to choose the MOST correct. Very seldom will you get an answer set where there is one obviously correct answer and three or four obviously incorrect answers. But academic researcher William Poundstone suggests in his research of M/C questions that you should NOT look for a pattern, as it is very unlikely any sort of pattern exists.

While strategies and suggestions for success on M/C exam questions vary wildly, I think it is best to the read the question and answer it BEFORE looking at the possible answers. While it is not ALWAYS possible to do this, you generally should try to answer the question before you look at the answer. Then, with your answer to the question in mind, look down at the possible answers and choose the one that most closely matches your thoughts on the question. This will keep you from over-analyzing the issue and becoming confused. Answer the question in your mind, pick the answer closest to what you think the answer should be, and move on. Do not second guess yourself.

Also, understand there is generally no 'secret pattern' or most likely answer, like 'C' every third time. There is likely NO PATTERN, so don't try to see one. Many professors, including me, utilize software which accompanies the text which generates M/C exam questions which have randomly generated answers, so any pattern is an illusion. This software can also arrange the questions to appear in a range of difficulty from easy to very hard. Please understand this is not always the case, and not all professors use the software available.

Another benefit of using this type of exam software is the ability to generate exams with the same questions which are randomly arranged for each recipient; each student then gets an almost unique exam which eliminates any benefit from memorizing a string of answers from someone who took the exam earlier in the day or who is sitting across the aisle. This software can also provide exams which cover exactly the same content, but which generate totally different M/C questions about the same concept, ensuring a totally unique exam for each student.

If you simply do not know the answer to a M/C question, leave it and move on. Do not waste time stressing over questions you cannot quickly answer. Sometimes the answer is found later on during the same exam in subsequent answers for other questions or even in subsequent questions. When finished with what you know, go back to those you did not know first time, and use your 'gut feeling.' If you recognize something, if you think this might be an answer, go with it. Since you don't really know the answer, a good guess is better than nothing.

William Poundstone, in his book *Rock Breaks Scissors*, reports on the findings of research regarding various strategies for common games like rock, paper, scissors and includes discussion of his findings and analysis of multiple choice (including T/F) exams. His most surprising finding for T/F questions was that professors in his sample of exams chose True as the correct answer 60% of the time. As I have always suggested to my students, he says to answer those questions for which you DO know the answer and move on, quickly skipping over those you are sure you DON'T know the answer to.

He then suggests, as I do, that you go back to those you did not answer, and look at your answers on either side of the question; presumably these would be answers you did know. He says when both answers on either side of the unknown are the same, guess the opposite on the unknown; this is particularly effective on T/F.

He also says that if the before and after answers are different, guess true. He found that B is the favored answer 28% of the time, when four answers are given as choices, and E is the favored answer 23% of the time when five answers are given as choices. The answer C is favored on M/C exams, being the correct choice only 17% of the time.

Poundstone's findings concur with my observations and suggestion to avoid answers that include never, always, all, or none, except when one of the answers is 'all of the above' or 'none of the above' for a fourth, fifth, or sixth possible answer for a M/C question; choose that if you are guessing.

Poundstone suggests another effective strategy for a guess for an unknown is to choose the answer that is the longest. He says that examiners want to make sure the answer is indisputably correct, so often they will include more qualifying language in the correct answer.

Breaking down the question: a case study

Below I present a case study of an actual student's preparation for what was to be an upcoming final during which I showed him how to break down a question; this provides another example to show you that process. He later thanked me and said this process worked brilliantly, making it easier to handle the exam in that class, but also just about any question he faced in other classes.

Here are the notes for final exam review questions provided by the professor for a logic class which one of our basketball players was going to face right after our time at the Western Athletic Conference basketball tournament.

Together, we studied the professor's exam preparation prompts which consisted of eight sample questions worth 100 points/marks in total. The allotted time would be two hours so we first created a theoretical plan for how he would spend his time. Based on the information provided, he had 120 minutes for 100 points. Off the top, this suggests he had at least 20 minutes to plan; using our rule of thumb for planning vs writing, he could commit up to 40 minutes total to planning, or about 4 minutes per question.

The planning process would result in a set of notes similar to the photo below which shows how to break down the question, including the components of the answer, how many sentences, and how much time to spend writing. You will see from the notes in the photo that the first question is worth 10 points; in the study materials provided, the professor wrote:

"The first question on the final exam will ask you to use a Venn diagram to analyze the validity of a categorical syllogism. 10 points."

In the next section, I will provide the details for actually breaking down this question which can serve as a model to use in your own examinations.

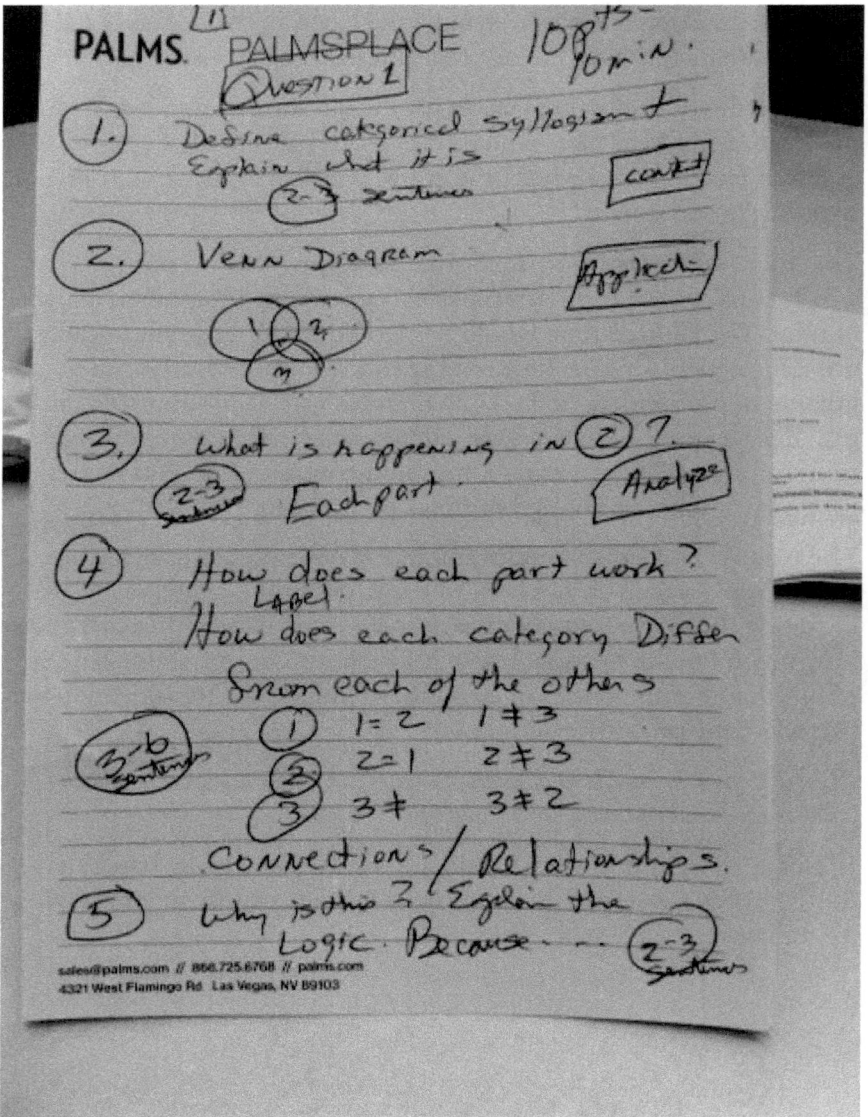

Case study: understand the question's 'command words'

In this case, the professor uses the command word "analyze" when he/she says you will be expected to 'analyze the validity of categorical syllogism.'

Case study: break down the question

The exam question tells us we need to be able to define categorical syllogism, and draw and explain a Venn diagram which is used to analyze categorical syllogism.

Once we broke down the parts of the question, we addressed each in detail. The professor did not provide any rubric or metric to use during the breakdown of the question; this is what I suggest from my own experience as an IB/A-Level teacher.

#1 Content. Define the applicable term/concept (categorical syllogism in this case) in two, no more than three, sentences. As I have stated more than once, you simply cannot succeed unless you absolutely have the vocabulary, terminology, and concepts covered in class down cold.

#2 Application. Draw the applicable diagram (in this case a Venn diagram) and label it correctly. As we can see, the Venn diagram has three intersecting circles; in addition to using identifiers within the diagram itself, any drawing or graph used to demonstrate your ability to apply a concept must be labeled accurately and completely and thoroughly explained.

If you are using a graph, you must be able to demonstrate that you understand how the graph works, which also means both the x and y axes are labeled correctly and the data points reflect what is actually happening. Generally, although not always, it is okay on an exam to have only a relatively accurate scale; it is not usually necessary to have exact scale and exact data points. Clarify with your professor before the exam if you are uncertain.

#3 Analysis. What is happening in #2 where you demonstrated application? Here you begin the analysis process by briefly explaining what each numbered circle represents.

#4 Analysis, continued. You then continue your analysis by explaining how each circle interacts with the others using 2 to 3 sentences to explain how each circle works individually and then how each circle differs from each of the other circles. This part explains the connections and relationships of the parts. So, as you can see in the picture, you first focus on circle 1, explaining what it represents and how it works individually, then you explain the relationship between 1 and 2 and between 1 and 3. Then you focus on circle 2, explaining what it represents and how it works individually, then explain the relationship between 2 and 1 and between 2 and 3. Then you focus on circle 3, explaining what it represents and how it works individually, then explain the relationship between 3 and 1 and between 3 and 2.

#5 Analysis, continued. Why is this? You conclude your answer to the question by explaining why. You best accomplish this by writing "because…" (followed by your reasoning) in 2-3 sentences, for each circle; you would spend about 2 minutes on each part. In this final section, you are confirming the validity of categorical syllogism by explaining or providing the answer to the question.

Of course, you could answer the question by simply completing that last sentence. Although the professor MIGHT reward you, I am pretty sure a one sentence answer will garner you only one or two points.

Case study: how to spend your time on this question.

- In total, you would spend about 3 minutes breaking down this question, formulating a written plan similar to the example in the photo.

- Then you would spend 7 to 8 minutes writing approximately 17-26 sentences and drawing one diagram

- #1 spend no more than a minute writing no more than a couple of sentences defining categorical syllogism and Venn diagram

- #2 spend about 1 minute drawing and labeling the Venn diagram

- #3 spend no more than 2 minutes writing 2-3 sentences for each circle completing the first part of the analysis which is approximately 6 sentences for this section

- #4 spend another 2 minutes writing 2-3 sentences for each circle to continue the analysis which is approximately 6 sentences for that section

- #5 to conclude, spend another couple of minutes writing 3-5 sentences confirming the validity of categorical syllogism, which serves as the answer to the question

Again, there is no shortcut; content knowledge is a prerequisite to breaking down the question and answering it in an acceptable way. Using this sample exam question as an example, if you really don't know what a Venn diagram is and you don't understand categorical syllogism, there is not much you can do to get a passing score on the exam.

Some final thoughts on exams: grading, marks, and scoring

Please understand that there is no way I can know exactly and specifically what your professor is looking for. However, there is a basic hierarchy that almost all teachers/professors follow in grading exams and papers. Generally speaking, your score is almost always a combination of grammar, spelling, content knowledge, application, analysis and evaluation. I offer four specific writing skills which must be addressed in order to get better scores or marks from the professor.

Your essay/paragraph must be constructed correctly with thesis, support, and examples, and your sentences should be grammatically correct. This means you need to avoid run-on sentences, sentence fragments, misspelled words, and comma faults; you need to have clear pronoun reference; you need to be aware of preposition placement; you need to have a consistent point of view AND tense through the entire paper. Of course, this is not a complete list, but rather a reminder to pay attention to structure, grammar and spelling.

Passing an exam which is entirely Multiple Choice is relatively straightforward since there is a correct answer for each question. But an exam which includes questions requiring a written answer requires additional skills. When scoring a written exam, the teacher/professor generally has a rubric and looks for key points, concepts, and terms while reading the answer. If you put your answer into a logical order following the example given, it will be easier for the teacher to grade and will likely result in a higher score for you. It is my belief that teachers actually do want you to succeed and will strive to give you the benefit whenever possible. It is really in your best interest if you make it easier rather than harder for your teacher to do this.

In order to simply pass the written exam, you must demonstrate an understanding of the concepts in the syllabus, including formulae, terms and definitions. The minimum most teachers/professors require of students in order to pass is to provide evidence of understanding; this requires you to write down the correct answer along with the appropriate formula, theory, ratio, or concept to define the problem and possible solution.

However, as we likely know, simply passing the exam might not be enough to ensure that you get the score you need to maintain progress to graduation, or eligibility or admission to university. To increase your score, you generally must demonstrate skill in Application, which includes the calculation of the math to arrive at an accurate answer, the use of correct and relevant concepts, content, and knowledge within the context of the case study, question, article, or problem. To further strengthen your answer, you generally have to demonstrate skill in analysis. The best answer will include all of the above AND generally demonstrate an ability to evaluate; this might be done implicitly, but it must be done if the question explicitly requires it.

Conclusion

One of the pleasures of being a teacher or coach is when a student actually tells you about something valuable he/she learned in that educational or athletic endeavor in which you were both involved.

Recently, a university student home on break shared that perhaps the most valuable thing she got out of my economics class was not the economic theory, although that probably helped her to do better in the course than otherwise would have been possible. To her, the most valuable thing she learned was how to break down a question. This one thing, something taken as granted by most professors and taught by so few teachers, brought about her success more than anything. Yes, it is relatively simple, but my purpose here is to help you to realize that even a simple question has many layers and once you understand HOW to deal with an exam question, your life will become just that much easier.

The next two chapters provide additional information affecting your ability to handle exams. To be successful, you will need to understand what the command words mean and how to address them and you will need to understand the concepts of analysis and evaluation and how to assimilate them into your work.

Chapter 14
Understanding
Analysis and Evaluation

What is analysis?

The women's basketball team met with me, in the team room, for one of our regularly scheduled academic weight room sessions.

We were talking about the importance of command words in an exam question, specifically analysis, and other words which imply the need to analyze. I asked for someone to explain analysis, and a varied though not completely accurate discussion ensued as different players offered their own idea of what it is.

Most had some idea, but to clarify the concept, I explained that they experienced analysis every time they saw the scouting report the coaches prepared for an upcoming opponent. A scouting report includes the first impressions of the opponent, the broad expectations for the upcoming game, and the key points of attack both offensively and defensively. The coach generally diagrams the offensive sets and includes video to show exactly how the play is run, the sequence of events, and what is likely going to happen.

Often, another coach will then go into extensive detail on the opposition's best players. For example, analytical evidence of the top scorer's characteristics might show a slow, high dribble is the key indicator of the player's rhythmic preparation for a three point shot while the lower quick dribble indicates an impending move toward the lane or basket. Knowing these tendencies gives the defensive player a chance to better handle that move when they see that particular behavior tipping off that offensive player's intent. Identifying those tendencies along with the salient components of the opponent's offensive and defensive schemes is accomplished through analysis. This example of analysis in daily life enabled me to help the student athletes have a better understanding of the academic skill of analysis.

So what is analysis? The dictionary defines analysis as a systematic series of actions with which you study the nature of something or determine its essential features and their relationships.

When you analyze data, or outcomes, or a play, or a game film, you are figuring out how something works or what the numbers are telling you. You then continue analysis as you try to establish as many connections to other data, variables and factors as possible. You are looking for trends, trying to compare the performance against a baseline or metric, trying to ascertain the probability that the possible problem is in fact a likely culprit, and looking at alternative solutions and the likelihood of success.

The most common type of analysis occurs when you are given a chart or graph from which you have to figure out and explain what is happening. Indeed, an investment banker is primarily an analyst, trying to figure out what the financial statements of the company are telling investors. The analyst in this case is using known ratios and general rules of thumb to guide any decision to buy or to sell.

In basketball, we do the same thing with the statistics we have collected about our own performance as well as those of our opponents. We do a macro analysis into general coaching style or philosophy. For example, is the team going to push the pace, use pressure defense, and try to maximize the number of shots? Or are they going to slow it down and extend every possession as long as possible to shorten the game? Then we will do a micro analysis, which looks to figure out the tendencies for every player, time and situation tendencies for the team, and specific plays and patterns they will run including the likely scenario for each.

Once you have done your own macro analysis of an exam question and your own answer, you dig down by asking *why* to identify unintended consequences, underlying problems, and hidden causes for the cause and effect relationships you previously identified.

Analysis and reading

I wrote about how to do a quick read in Chapter 10. As part of your BC routine, a quick read is a strategy to help you prepare for the upcoming lecture, to begin the process of understanding the material. While a quick read is a valuable tool, it simply does not enable you to get to a deeper meaning of the text, which is required in both shared inquiry classrooms and in most upper level humanities and social studies courses. To do this requires a deep read, during which you necessarily do an analysis of what you are reading.

This deep read requires that you read the text thoroughly. It also means you are likely going to read the text more than once, perhaps several times, in order to understand it well enough to answer the questions you are posing during the analysis.

Christina Hank Collins (@ChristinaHank) says deep reading is analysis, that it is an outcome rather than a strategy. To do this type of analysis, she says you must read paragraph-by-paragraph, sentence-by-sentence, and word by word to determine the purpose of each paragraph, sentence, or word. Words matter and one of your goals, in a deep read, is to figure out how meaning can be altered when key words are changed; only through a deep read can you determine why the author chose one word over another.

In a series of blog posts, Grant Wiggins also makes the point that deep reading is analysis and he provides a few key characteristics which identify what this looks like. When doing a deep read, you analyze the information by observing and noting the facts and details about which you then ask some questions. What does this information mean to you? What do these facts tell you? What is your take on this? When you add up all the facts, what do they tell you?

You are also undertaking analysis when you pick apart the author's main points; of course, you must figure out what these are, and then you ask another series of questions about his/her text. What is the argument? What is the author's point? Why does it matter? Is it relevant? Does it make sense to you? Why or why not?

During a Socratic Seminar training, Bill Cathers introduced participants to the book *How to Read* by Mortimer Adler. It has been in my collection for several years, and I have tried to assimilate its instruction into my own life as well as that of my students. Adler says there is elementary reading, followed by skimming (quick reading), and then the skill of analytical reading. He and co-author Charles Van Doren devote five chapters to analysis, but not all information in all chapters is applicable to my point. To actually accomplish deep reading from a curricular standpoint, it is likely necessary to learn how to suspend judgement but I only want share the more accessible take-aways related to your ability to analyze.

When doing a deep read, you must first try to figure out the author's theme; Adler discusses this in Chapter 7, entitled *X-Raying a Book*. Then you must read more deeply, repeatedly if necessary, to get to the author's main idea, argument, or assertion. This requires that you understand the terms, vocabulary, and keywords before trying to figure out the author's message. Once you have done this, you can then offer your own take on what the author said. To this end, you answer questions like these: Does the author make any sense to me, either personally, or in the context of the book as an analogy or allegory, or as a solution to a problem? Does the book and the author's message matter? Why is the author making his/her point? Is it important to know this information? Why or why not?

Analysis is not being skeptical of something and it is not being a doubter of research findings or scientific data. I think that sometimes people take an opposing position, or a devil's advocate stance, as a way to create an impression that he/she has actually done some analysis of a situation (or a document or story or something said by a candidate).

Deep reading and the necessary accompanying analysis takes time and effort. You will want to, in fact you will need to, engage this skill of deep reading of text as a way to analyze a situation, to figure out what is going on, whether it is in your classes, as part of an assignment or in your personal life. Indeed, sorting through the myriad of blatantly false claims and texts posted on our various social networks and analyzing everything else is something that every thinking person needs to be able to accomplish on a daily basis in order to be not only a successful student, but a productive member of society.

Analysis and poetry

Think back to the story I told earlier about the student whose mother thought she did poorly on the exam because she had never seen that poem before. And my retort was that it would be impossible for the teachers of English poetry to explicitly teach every possible poem. Instead, I encouraged the teachers to embrace the idea of teaching students how to break down, or analyze, any poem or question rather than striving to memorize correct answers. I am not an English teacher, but my own education suggests an analytical model that should enable most students to be relatively successful, if required, when interpreting poetry on an exam or class assignment.

When analyzing a poem, you are digging into the layers. First, you read the poem, circling words you don't understand. As I said earlier, it is almost impossible to analyze something if you don't understand the vocabulary. If you are not in an exam, you look up the meaning. If you are in the exam, you have to figure out what the word means by studying the context; what is the likely overall meaning of the passage in question, which then provides you with some hints as to the word's meaning.

Then you work to uncover three layers; while professors have sometimes disparaged this 'group of three' model, it is my contention that for students who have no model to utilize, the three argument or three layer model is a great place to start.

Your goal for layer one would be to identify the literal meaning of the poem. The literal meaning would be your first impression on what is happening in the poem, what the words seem to mean, without trying to see hidden meaning in the plot, actions or words. Once you have a basic, perhaps superficial, idea of the meaning of the poem, you then try to figure out the poem's hidden meaning. This is an interpretation so there is not necessarily a right or wrong answer, but it is likely the professor will want you to recognize the generally accepted hidden meaning. Most poems have been analyzed in every conceivable way and most then have hidden meaning(s) that are generally accepted and then presented as knowledge to students in secondary education.

When you look for hidden meaning, try to figure out if there are words that can be used a second way, which have a second meaning that then changes the entire poem. Are there words that create a picture in your mind? Are there words that create a strong emotional pull? This level is figurative, meaning you are looking for something the words seem to represent rather than what the words literally are in the first level.

The third layer, to me, is how the words flow and the images created by the words resonate in an almost musical fashion. When analyzing the poem to get into this third layer of meaning, you are trying to identify the pace or rhythm the poet is using, which he/she creates through the structure of the work. This might be something as simple as rhyme and rhythm, which are techniques the poet uses to help the poem move forward, enhance meaning, and to help the words work together. Or he/she might use alliteration, or use repeated consonant sounds to create an aural or musical rhythm.

At this third level, you are also contemplating the power of lyrics and music working together to create a deeper connection and provide a deeper meaning in the way a song can profoundly impact us. Do the lyrics or words strike a chord? When the words in a poem resonate, the simple analogy is that they strike a chord. In music, a chord is three or more notes that, when hit at the same time, blend harmoniously. So even though you are not actually hearing musical notes, the words you read cause your synapses to fire as if responding to music. This effect creates an emotional attachment and often improves your mood, but also makes the poem easier to remember and recite due to its profound meaning and its impact upon you. Could this poem be set to music? Is it musical in nature by itself? Is it a lyric that has previously been set to music? For example, Van Morrison's lyrics have been compiled into a collection of poetry called *Keep It Lit*.

The three-layer model helps you understand content, or the fundamental message of the work. It also helps you to formulate your interpretation of the poet's intent and his/her techniques. Once you have dug into the three layers, you might then talk about the poem's tone, whether the poet is striking a light mood, or a dark heavy feeling and how he/she accomplished this. Then you would address the technique used in each layer. Your English teacher would expect you to know specific techniques a poet might use. For example, you would most likely need to understand and explain how the poet uses figurative language such as imagery, alliteration, and onomatopoeia to not only create images in your mind but also appeal to your senses of taste, touch, smell, and hearing. You also would be expected to address techniques such as rhyme, alliteration, rhythm, and repetition, which help to create a beat or meter that helps you to move with the poet, creating a feeling which helps you to better understand what he/she is trying to do with the work. Because every poem is deeper than its apparent meaning, you will want to be aware of, and understand, the common techniques used.

From this three-layer analysis model, along with the consideration of technique, you should be in a pretty good position to answer exam questions and support a position regarding your interpretation of that poem. Remember, it is one model you can utilize so you don't find yourself wondering what to do if you have never seen the poem before.

I think most English teachers do teach how to analyze a poem and will likely provide a model of their own design, but it is possible yours did not. If you missed or forgot that portion of your English class, this approach to breaking down a poem will at least minimally serve your needs. In the end, analysis is the process of asking questions and digging into the layers; it is a skill you can learn and one which is adaptable across many disciplines.

Analysis and writing your exam essay

The score the teacher or professor awards for your written response to a question (or for an essay you have written) will be determined in large part by your skill in analysis. Recognizing that there was more to success in a course and school than content knowledge, I spent time in class explaining not only what application, analysis, and evaluation are, but also how to apply, analyze, and evaluate the question, problem, or topic as well as your own answer or position. As I talked about analysis and how to analyze, I drew a cryptic picture of a typical silver mine (Aspen was one of the leading silver mining towns in the United States in the late 1800's and the area is still marked with evidence of that mining history), with several vertical levels on the board.

I explained the top, upper level was the top, most superficial answer to the question. Analysis requires the student to dig deeper; each subsequent level was a 'why' question such as why does it matter? Or why does it work this way? Or why is this? This then led to another 'why is that' question and answer. I suggested that students needed to dig down at least three levels in order to show any semblance of analysis.

Chapter 14

In my IB Business course, I talked about the need to identify exactly what the problem is before trying to figure out possible solutions. Many students are proficient in problem solving if they have been told what the problem is. However, I think a significant issue exists in school and in business regarding a student's or a worker's ability to identify exactly what the problem is in the first place, let alone how to solve it.

It is harder to solve a problem that you have not yet identified, just as it is harder to answer a question that you have not seen before. Analysis is a required skill for identifying and solving problems. And one of the key words that can be used to help figure out the problem is 'why.'

In her article *The Formula to Better Problem Solving*, Courtney Seiter says the "Five Whys" technique will help you get to the root of any problem. This problem solving technique comes from Toyota, which included it as the critical component of their problem solving training. According to Seiter, the originator was Taichi Ohono, who described the method as the "basis of Toyota's scientific approach...by repeating why five times, the nature of the problem as well as the solution becomes clear."

A simple example I used for my students went something like this:

1. *Why were you late for class?* I got stopped on way to school for speeding.

2. *Why were you speeding?* My alarm did not go off, so I got up late, and needed to hurry to get to school on time.

3. *Why did the alarm not work?* My phone was dead.

4. *Why is the phone dead?* I did not plug it in to charge.

5. *Why did you not plug it in?* I only have one charger and I left it at school in my locker.

What is the solution? Another charger to leave at home.

Of course, sometimes it does not go as smoothly. Another student was having difficulty in class and her grade had plummeted to an uncharacteristically low level. I asked her about this (but we only got 4 'whys' in):

1. *Do you have any idea why your grade is way below your norm?* I haven't been studying as much as I used to.

2. *Why are you not studying as much?* I have to work every night.

I thought this was odd; why did she have to work every night? The decline in grades had certainly coincided with a relatively new job, but it did not appear she needed to work. Of course, looks can be deceptive, but at the risk of getting too personal, I went ahead and asked,

3. *Why do you need to work?* I need to pay for my car.

4. *Okay, but why do you need a car?* (considering the distance to school was easily bikeable and a very efficient bus service stopped just outside). I laughed when she said, I need a car to get to work.

This is an example of a circular argument; there is no apparent reason for the job other than to get a car, which is needed to get to work. Nevertheless, in most cases the why analytical technique is an effective tool in the problem solving process. And not only is this skill or technique valuable for those interested in a career in business, we can adapt it when answering exam questions and writing essays.

When conducting analysis, you will need to work on both sides of the question; first, you will break down the data related to the problem or case to determine its significance. You are trying to figure out what data is important, what is not, and why. Then you will work on the answer side, conducting the same scrutiny on your answer. So when a command word (see Chapter 15) for an exam question or an assigned essay or paper requires (or implies) the skill of analysis, you begin the process by asking Why, What, and How. These simple questions help you to identify cause and effect relationships and connections, which is the fundamental goal of analysis. Once you have done some analysis, you are then able to evaluate.

What is evaluation?

The examination process will inevitably include command words which imply or require evaluation. Questions that begin 'evaluate,' 'assess,' 'critically assess,' 'discuss,' 'determine the extent to which,' or 'to what extent' require you to show the skill of evaluation in order to reach the highest achievement levels.

When you demonstrate skill in evaluation, you make an appraisal of a situation, weigh (explain, describe, rank) the evidence available, and discuss the convincing aspects of an argument as well as any implications and limitations. Once you have identified the pros and cons, you then exercise judgement about where the argument seems to weigh in, or which side seems to have the most compelling argument or preponderance of support.

How to demonstrate skill in evaluation

When factors such as causes, consequences, or remedies are asked for, you must list at least three, attempt to rank the most important and then justify the reason for your choice.

When evaluating pros and cons, or advantages and disadvantages, you will need to identify and list three pros and rank them in order of importance, then identify and list three cons and rank them in order of importance, then choose which side, the pro or con, seems to have the advantage. You then support this position with two or three pieces of evidence, or reasons, for your support. This support should not be opinion, but rather evidence taken from the reading or from what you learned in class.

When you are asked to evaluate possible strategies to be used in a situation, you must identify and assess the pros and cons of the strategies in the same way I detailed above. You must also add a discussion of both the short term and long term implications (benefits and costs).

When data is presented in a chart or graph or spreadsheet, evaluation occurs when you check on the validity of that data in terms of whether it is appropriate, whether it is reliable, or whether it is still relevant. In an examination, not all data is applicable, so part of the evaluation process is determining what data is actually important to the question. Sometimes students think that just because it is included in the documentation, or as part of the question, it must all be used. Not necessarily. You must use your judgement to figure out whether the data or information matters (or not) before you can even think about the validity of the data or information you choose to use or apply.

You observation about the validity of the data must be based on research or other data which supports or refutes the data in question. You cannot simply offer an opinion about the validity of the data and expect that opinion to be accepted and respected.

Evaluation is not absolute. I think you are better served to use words such as *perhaps*..... or *may*.....or *might*..... or *however*......or *on the one hand this, but on the other hand that*, rather than use words that convey an absolute certainty such as will, must, always, never. When you evaluate, you are measuring and judging how something relates to, and compares to, something else; in most cases, relationships are multivariate.

Evaluation often includes a ranking. It would be appropriate to include a last, short, paragraph (2-3 lines) where there is some attempt to rank/assess what you have written. For example, you should write something along the lines: It seems that (given the particulars of the case/question) the most significant or appropriate ..... effect or, result or, benefit or, cost or, policy .....is xxxxx because ...... (mention the two or three most significant reasons).

Conclusion

This chapter was designed to help you better understand what the teacher or professor is talking about when they say you must analyze or evaluate.

Inherent in that understanding is what command words used in a question mean. A significant argument of this book is the contention that many of the issues causing students difficulty in college are really a function of the words used by professors, the expectation the professor has, and the presumption by the professor that the students understand what is being said. Often it is the case that students, even those in graduate school, don't really understand terms and directions.

The next chapter talks in detail about command words commonly used in examination questions.

Chapter 15
Understanding
Command Words

"I nailed the exam."

A student brought me a graded exam which the professor had returned for the student to review. The student was visibly upset by her grade and particularly frustrated because she felt that she had done very well on the exam; indeed, she told me right after taking the exam "I nailed the exam." So, we spent the rest of our appointment going over the exam questions and her corresponding answers.

The first question asked the student to simply define a concept; she provided a correct definition in two sentences, but made the mistake of providing an additional five sentences of explanation. The question was worth 2 points, and the professor awarded her those points. The additional five sentences simply wasted time.

The second question asked her to use a graph to explain what was happening is a hypothetical scenario presented in the question worth 8 points. She provided an accurate graph, but failed to label it and her explanation was general in nature, lacking specifics. The professor awarded her 5 of 8 points.

So far, she had a C.

The next question contained a command word that required her to demonstrate the skill of analysis and was worth 12 points. This would indicate a need for about 12 sentences exploring cause and effect, causal connections, or how something came to be. She wrote 5 sentences, getting started in the analysis but not providing enough depth, for which the professor awarded her 8 points. At that point, she had accumulated 15 of 32 points.

The final question asked her to determine the extent to which a policy change would benefit or harm a constituency and was worth

18 points. She gave a valiant effort and wrote 10 to 12 sentences, for which the professor generously awarded her 13 points. In the end, she received a (barely) passing grade of D- on the exam and was faced with a steep uphill climb to improve the grade.

The issue, however, was not that she did not know the terms, but that she did not fully understand how to handle the command terms embedded in the question. When you take a summative exam, it is crucial that you understand these command words and how much you will need to write for each before you sit the exam, as you will not have a chance to show subsequent improvement.

Understanding the question's 'command words'

These command words are structured on my interpretation of the revised Bloom's Taxonomy Model and are presented in order from lower level/least complicated to higher level/most complicated in the categories 1 through 5 below. Each category has an identifier.

- Category 1 is Knowledge, or simply your ability to memorize or remember.

- Category 2 is Comprehension, or understanding, and is your ability to interpret or paraphrase what you just read.

- Category 3 is Application, or your ability to demonstrate problem solving.

- Category 4 is Analysis, or the ability to break something down into component parts.

- Category 5 is Evaluation.

Generally speaking, the more complicated the command word (meaning it comes from a higher taxonomy level) the more you have to write. Usually, an exam has a set of questions that range from category 1 to category 5; from least difficult to most difficult. If there is only one question, it is quite likely the answer will require you to address all five levels in the answer. If you embrace this hierarchy, you can see that a person who is capable of only category 1 command words MIGHT pass with a D, but unless you are capable of all five categories, you simply cannot get an A.

I am presenting a general understanding of the command words; however, it is possible your specific professor might have a slightly different take on a given word. In the end, if you can differentiate between these words by using this guide, you will be far better off than if you don't clearly understand the differences. Not all possible command words are defined or exemplified in this chapter but they are a sample of the words my own students have had trouble with (including the student in the opening story of this chapter).

Category 1 command words come from the lowest level of the widely used Bloom's Taxonomy and serve as the basis for the easiest questions you will encounter. These command words require you to simply recall and write down the information. When you answer a question driven by this type of command word, it is not considered to be reflective of 'higher order thinking skills' and questions of this type are usually worth fewer points. A few words you might see which examine your knowledge are discussed next.

Define. This word asks you to explain the meaning of a term from class, requiring you to provide a precise definition of a given word or concept. Be sure to stay within the context of the question or case, as some terms have a couple of correct definitions, depending upon the context or situation. Write only one or two sentences as this command simply requires content recall and application to the question.

What. This word asks you to clarify a situation, or a term, or a concept. It also might ask you to demonstrate your basic understanding of an idea or concept, as in "what is money?"

Category 2 command words come from the lower-middle taxonomy level which measures understanding and are of average difficulty. They ask you to clearly explain ideas or concepts. Some of the words you might see used in exam questions – designed to measure understanding – are discussed next.

Compare. This means you need to describe two situations and present similarities and differences. You are expected to recognize the similarities between the two as well as the differences. Therefore, simple descriptions of the two situations does not meet the requirements of this key word.

Describe. Sometimes used in questions to determine knowledge, it is more a word to ascertain your understanding and invites you to provide your take on a given situation; it is your observation and an accompanying written descriptive picture of what you think is happening. You will not be expected to provide any sort of critical review or analysis, so don't spend time doing this as you will not be rewarded.

Discuss. This word asks you consider both sides of an argument. You will be expected to address each point presented in the data, or question, and offer an observation on the point. I recommend you use the key position/thesis model. With this approach, you articulate the key position(s) or thesis and offer three arguments of support for the position(s). You are not supporting an opinion, but rather supporting a position that is evidenced by the data in the case. When you engage in a discussion, you are recognizing the different views or points, and offering your input on each. Often, a discussion is a review of the situation, work, or case, which you conduct for the benefit of the reader.

Distinguish. This command word asks you to briefly identify and list the key the differences between two things, terms, or concepts. Generally, this type of question asks you to clarify your understanding of two similar terms, which are often confused. This serves as a screening tool for the teacher; he/she can easily determine who really knows what they are talking about and those who don't. In economics, for example, it is good to know if someone can quickly and easily distinguish between the government debt and the government deficit, or even more confusingly, between the government debt and the government debt ceiling.

Explain. This word invites you to make understandable a concept or idea. Imagine you are talking to someone who has not a clue what you are talking about. From this, you then take the opportunity to use words from the course, which you then clarify with synonyms that clarify the listener's understanding. You can also provide an example as long as the example is in the same context as the words used in the question.

Outline. This term is generally used in the context of art or drawing. In your class, a professor usually requires you to offer a brief summary of the major aspects of a situation. To do this, write two sentences for each point you make. The first sentence will be the point and the second will be for your analysis (basically saying 'why?' the point is important). If the question is worth 5 marks, make three points explained by two sentences each, or about 6 sentences in total; an exhaustive description is not required. Often, a question which asks you to outline the situation is simply asking for a broad overview of the situation.

Category 3 command words measure application and are from the middle taxonomy level. While they look simple, they are actually relatively difficult. Not only do they explicitly require you to use the correct formula, graph, or chart, they ask you to apply the information in a way the professor asks, which might be new to you. A few words you might see which examine your ability to apply are discussed next.

Articulate. This word asks you to put into writing an understanding of a process. For example, you might be asked to explain how a formula works, including its components and what it is designed to measure. This might also include rule of thumb benchmarks used for answers derived from commonly used formulae.

Calculate. The word asks you to find a precise answer using a mathematical process you learned in class. There is only one acceptable answer, and you are generally expected to show your work.

Illustrate. This is not necessarily asking you to draw a diagram. But a diagram is probably useful and will help you to better clarify what you are talking about when you provide an example from your own experience (or a professor's lecture). In some cases, the directive to illustrate is an explicit request for you to demonstrate your understanding by drawing a diagram or graph.

Category 4 command words are more difficult and come from the upper-middle taxonomy level. These words ask you to analyze a case or data attached to your exam or distinguish between the different parts of the question. Regardless of the term used to invite your analysis, you will be expected to explain the cause/effect relationship of those parts/components and explain why. A few words you might see which examine your ability to analyze are discussed next.

Analyze. This is not an opinion, but rather a detailed argument which shows and explains cause and effect. To do this, you must look at the detail of the data and make the connection between that data and what seems to be happening; you are identifying the outcome(s) and reasons for (why?) that outcome. Make sure you mention and assess the consequences of your conclusion. Analysis divides things into parts; in an analysis, you are breaking down the problem or case study into component parts, which sometimes are not explicitly stated. When you break a problem or question or case down into component parts, you will explore and explain each part and how it contributes to the overall meaning you are trying to convey. This overall meaning is your thesis about the situation, which must be stated in the first paragraph of the answer you write.

Explain why. Again, this is not an opinion. To explain why, you must first ask the question 'why?' of yourself. Then write your answer with detailed reasoning. The best model would probably be the thesis/position plus two or three points of data support, followed by a conclusion.

Examine the extent. This is a form of analysis which means to identify the extent, make 2-3 arguments in support of that position

Why. This short command word seems so elementary, but it is key to almost every question and essay, as it is a way to initiate the process of analysis. 'Why' invites you to present reasons for the existence of something.

Compare and contrast. This is very similar to compare, where you have to recognize similarities and differences, but with contrast you add an *analysis* of the differences between the two topics. This means you talk about the obvious, but you also must spend time parsing out less obvious, or hidden characteristics. And with any type of analysis, you are required to ask and answer the question 'why?'

Category 5 command words come from the upper taxonomy level and are the most difficult. Evaluation is a careful and reasoned judgement of the value or condition of an action, proposal, or position. A few words you might see which examine your ability to evaluate are discussed next.

Account for. The command word requires you to undertake careful consideration of the case, document, reading, or data and present a reasoned case for the existence of something in that information at a given point in time. This also requires you to write about what you think are the reasons, motives, or causes for an action that has been taken or which has occurred.

Assess. This word is similar to evaluate and requires you to make a judgment about something. It is not simply an opinion, but rather a recognition of the positions for and against followed by a conclusion based on the strength of evidence. On which side does the evidence seem to come down? I allowed, and I argue that other teachers and professors are willing to allow, assessments which differed from the marking rubric as long as the student presented a strong argument accompanied by solid reasoning for their conclusion.

Evaluate. This command word requires you to thoughtfully and logically judge the value, significance, or condition of a position, proposal, idea, or solution. To present this opinion and reasoned judgment, you do not say that it is your opinion; instead you talk about both sides of the topic, providing two or three points of support or evidence for each, followed by your judgement about where the evidence, or greatest support, seems to lie. Evaluation answers relate to implied questions such as "Is this reasonable... accurate... ethical... useful... compelling... comprehensive... important... what it seems to be?" You can use a 'for/against/why?' or 'pro/con/conclusion' case study mode or you might choose to use a 'position' model which requires you to state your position followed by 2-3 arguments of support. Then each of those 2 or 3 arguments is supported with 2 or 3 arguments or paragraphs. Either way, your conclusion must be connected to your position by data from the question, as well as knowledge from the course, along with connections you make with real situations in the world today.

Justify. When you justify, you provide reasons for (or show) that something is good, just, or right. This is an opinion which requires a fully-reasoned argument in support. Similar to evaluate, but more detailed, this fully reasoned argument is logical and well connected to data and information from either the case or course.

Recommend. When writing a recommendation, you are trying to convince the reader to support something or someone you like. When writing an answer to a question asking you to recommend, I suggest you use the for/against/conclusion model. You arrive at a position or recommendation only through: detailed analysis of the data and logical reasoning of cause and effect in which you identify both sides of the issue. Then, you conclude with sound judgement justified or supported by detailed arguments which reflect two or three levels of connections to the case in question. This type of exam question would test all skills: knowledge, content, application, analysis, and evaluation. It requires that you make connections within the case as well as connections to larger concerns.

To what extent, or **Determine the extent to which**. This wording requires serious and careful reflection and deep understanding of the situation. The wording implies that the question and topic is one where there is a debate of some kind, requiring you to give a judgement regarding the strength of opposing views about the facts surrounding a situation, or the credibility of a given position. Essentially, you want to weigh or measure each view on a relative scale; hence, the extent that each view weighs in on the topic based on your weighted analysis and evaluation of each.

Conclusion

This instruction about command words was developed from documents I received during A-Level and IB professional development as well as information shared by peers at the IBO curriculum center which I aligned with my own understanding and use of Bloom's Taxonomy. This chapter evolved directly from a document I shared with students in many of my classes.

Like the student in the opening story of this chapter, too many students had a misunderstanding of the command words, which simply caused incomplete answers and lower marks. I found their performance improved once they learned about, and distinguished between, these terms and I am confident this is a relatively simple academic skill you can embrace to improve your own scores on exam questions and essays.

The next chapter provides you with an easy-to-use essay structure applicable to almost every written exam question, essay, or paper you are required to write.

Chapter 16
An Essay Structure
that Improves your
Efficiency

Background Story

A student enrolled in the course 'Drugs and Society' was given an assignment to research and write about some aspect of the war on drugs. She said to me in a study session, "I don't know where to begin." So I asked what her title was. She said, "The War on Drugs."

Hmmm. That's a pretty broad topic. Was there any sort of direction from the professor? No. I suggested it would help if she directed her attention onto one specific aspect of the war on drugs. She seemed unsure of how to proceed, so I said, "Let's do this: Create a question as your title." She had never heard of that before, but I took this opportunity to share with her the technique I learned from another IB teacher, which I shared with my high school students for several years.

I asked her what her big idea was, what she wanted to say about the war on drugs. She indicated that she thought the overall result caused more problems than it solved. With that in mind, I helped her develop a three-part question, which she then used as a template to direct her writing toward an answer to the question: "To what extent has the war on drugs and supply interdiction, used to reduce the flow of illegal drugs into the U.S., benefited society."

With this title, she was then able to focus her attention on three things:

- what the war on drugs is trying to accomplish,

- the difference between supply interdiction and demand reduction,
- and finally the cost/benefit analysis.

With this in place, the student was able to create a framework relatively quickly, do the necessary research, and put together a reasonably strong paper by deadline.

Strategy for writing the essay

This chapter is designed to help you understand two strategies that provide a structure for writing an essay which can be broadly and relatively easily applied across disciplines and used for exam essays, homework essays, and multi-page extended essays and research papers.

My experience suggests that many students have difficulty starting an essay, so they just write things down, hoping inspiration hits; or they sit there, complaining they don't know what to say or how to start.

The solution is an easy to remember structure that makes it simple enough to plug and play. I was told by a professor that this standard model is too rudimentary for university students, but many students don't have an understanding of a viable structure at all, and the simplicity of the structure can be upgraded to a more complex model without changing the basics.

Assimilating this structure into my daily writing habits was an integral objective of English 601, a course required for my Master's degree. I offer a summary of my learning here as a way to help both university and high school students who perhaps missed coursework similar to this, or have forgotten the specifics from that course.

To effectively and efficiently write an essay or research paper, follow the steps and apply the details I present for you in the rest of the chapter.

Step 1. Understand the question or the professor's prompt

Analyze the question provided by the professor or teacher, or create your own question, both of which serve as a roadmap of sorts to guide your essay. This careful reading of the question requires you to reword the explicit question, or create a question implied in the prompt or topic in order to identify the three or four key ideas or concepts which you will need to address. If the question is implied, you will need to create a three-part question.

Often you are provided with an explicit question to write about. But what if you are given a broad topic instead, with perhaps only an implied question? As the student above did, many students simply title a paper or an essay with a general topic name or create an interesting-sounding collection of words which more or less try to give the professor or teacher a general idea about the paper.

However, a title framed as a question will make it easier for you to write your paper. At the very least, create a question related to your thesis which starts with why or how or to what extent. But a three-part question forces you to focus on the answer because this model necessarily leads you into a three-part answer as you develop the components of the paper.

Of course, not all papers or essays without an explicit instruction revolving around a question lend themselves well to a question, but research, position, and argument papers certainly do. It will be easier to write your paper if you answer a good three-part research question following this three-part model:

- Part 1: Concept/technique/tool as a Method or Process

- Part 2: Which is used in an attempt to fix a Problem

- Part 3: Resulting in an expected Result

A one-dimensional question serving as a title is better than one or two words, but it is still too broad to improve the student's writing efficiency and is not a viable guide for the student's subsequent essay. An example of a simple question as title would be "How can ABC Company improve its industrial relations?" On the other hand, this example of the three-part model which is derived from materials made available by and for IB instructors at the IBO curriculum center served as a guide for my IB Business and Management students. It differs from a how question because it leads the student sequentially into the three key concepts that need to be explained and/or discussed and allows for a specific answer or thesis to be addressed:

Question Part 1:

Method: ***Would non-monetary motivation methods***

Question Part 2:

Problem: ***reduce industrial relations problems***

Comment: Implicit analysis indicates the company has problems between the workforce and management/ownership. The first part of the question suggests non-monetary motivation might diminish or reduce those issues.

Question Part 3:

Expected result: ***while improving labor productivity at ABC Company?***

Comment: The final result of the non-monetary motivation would then be improved labor productivity due primarily to the improved relationship between labor and management.

Step 2. Plan your essay

Write down the three or four key points you identified in step 1, which are the ideas you need to address. These three key points, or ideas, will then lead to the answer for the question, problem, problem, or case.

From these three or four points, develop your thesis sentence and jot it down. The thesis is your one sentence summary of the answer to the question that you have been asked to answer (or the implied question you have created). A 'thesis' is your proposed answer to the question, the argument you are going to make, the possible solution to the problem.

From there, create a plan for your opening paragraph which serves as the guide for the reader. This thesis paragraph is a roadmap of sorts for both you and the instructor. Each sentence in the opening paragraph is a topic sentence, or thesis sentence, for subsequent paragraphs. If your essay title is a three-part question, the opening paragraph has a sentence for each part, plus a thesis, plus a transition.

A transition sentence links the paragraph you are currently completing with the key idea of the next paragraph you are going to write. When you transition from one paragraph to the next you will need to craft a sentence which includes a very short summary of the paragraph you are just finishing followed by a few words which provide a glimpse of the next paragraph. These transition sentences contain key words, which signal your intent to the reader.

To help explain the nature of transition sentences, I have included a few of these key words in eight categories. They are my interpretation and could differ from another instructor's.

1. Similarity. If the next paragraph is an additional argument or another explanation that is very close to the same thing you said in the paragraph you are working on, you would use words such as similarly or furthermore.

2. Sequential. If the argument, explanation, or description is in the form of a rank order or chronological order, you would use words such as next, then, or subsequently.

3. Time. If it is a matter of passing time, you would use words such as meanwhile, whenever, or once.

4. Contrast. When answering a question which includes a command word requiring that you contrast, or compare and contrast, you would use words such as however, nevertheless, on the other hand.

5. Example. When you have explained an idea or argument in the paragraph and wish to further explain through the use of an example, you would say for example, for instance, or to demonstrate.

6. Emphasis. When you want to add strength to your position or argument, you might use indeed or certainly.

7. Cause and effect. When you are writing an answer to a question requiring analysis, you will always attempt to establish the cause of an action and its subsequent effect. In doing this, you will likely have a paragraph identifying and explaining the cause followed by one which identifies and explains the effects on stakeholders. When you transition

between the two paragraphs, you would use the words consequently, therefore, or because.

8. Conclusion. Finally, you will get to the end of your explanation, analysis, and evaluation which requires you to tie things down. To transition to your final paragraph, use the words finally, in conclusion, or to summarize.

For an example of transition sentences, consider the question I talked about in Chapter 13:

The Bank of England (Central Bank for UK) Monetary Policy Committee will meet to discuss the economy and what action would be appropriate in response to this assessment. At this meeting they can do one of three things: A. raise interest rates; B. lower interest rates; C. leave interest rates where they are. What do you think they will do and why?

The question expects you to analyze what would likely happen when the bank raises interest rates, what would likely happen when they lower interest rates, and what would likely happen if the bank leaves interest rates where they are. At the very least, you would have three separate paragraphs explaining what is likely going to happen in each scenario and why, with a transition sentence between each. So, a sentence transitioning from your paragraph explaining (a) to a paragraph explaining (b) might be written similar to this:

> A BoE action to raise interest rates would likely cause the economy to contract, while on the other hand a BoE action to lower interest rates would likely create conditions for an expanding economy.

The second transition sentence would be one which moves you from the option (b) to option (c):

> While a BoE action to lower rates would expand the economy, they might instead choose to leave them alone because the economy has been relatively stable, with slight gains in the employment rate.

The third transition sentence for this question would be one where you move to your argument or position after you have explained the effect of the third option, which is leaving the interest rates be.

> While BoE action to leave interest rates as they are would extend the current stagnating economic conditions and rising rates could possibly cause a recession, it is my position that lowering rates would best serve the needs of most by encouraging conditions for an expanding and growing economy.

While still in the planning mode, decide what analysis and judgment/evaluation the question requires. If you are not sure about the requirements of your chosen question or that of the professor, check the chapter on command words. There is a good chance the essay question does require analysis because a good essay invariably includes both analysis and evaluation. Analysis is included in the body of the essay; you conduct analysis in each part of your essay based on the three or four point key points you have identified. In the evaluation, you present/discuss different viewpoints and then arrive at a conclusion based on where the data 'weighs in.'

The final step of the planning process is a broad outline or draft of the key points, which you will use to explain and support your position, answer, or solution. This draft includes your thesis, along with three or four points of support, and the key concept or theory from your text or class lecture, which leads you to the possible answer to the question or solution to the problem. If it is a quantitative problem, writing down the formula along with the theory is important.

Thoughts on the essay process

In any essay, two supported points are better than five minimally supported points or random pieces of information without support that might work.

Every time you write any answer, make the connection between what you know from the course and lectures, and what the question is asking. Link content together with connections to get a string of ideas, support, arguments, or reasons why. The best thing to do is to ask yourself the question *why* and proceed to explain why, for each point you make. The more you ask *why* and write that answer, the more depth you have. So, if you need to write a longer response, don't make more points, but delve deeper into the points you have already made by asking 'why' at each level. For every question, remember to address content, and application, and analysis, and evaluation.

Make a connection between content and context. This is application. Application is the ability to pick up the 2 or 3 concepts in the case, problem, article, or question, and use those concepts to develop the answer in the context of the question, case, article, or problem. For every question, you should be able to identify the concept(s) you are being asked to use, define, explain.

If you give an example, keep it in context of the course and the exam question. If, on the course, you have been talking about trade as an effective development strategy in Africa, don't use beef exports from California to Japan as an example.

Then you will need to analyze the question in the context of the course material. Analysis is connection between application/content and cause and effect relationships that you have identified in the case, question, or problem. Analysis is covered more completely in Chapter 14, but I want to remind you that you are demonstrating the depth of your understanding when you analyze.

Your essay will need to show evidence of your skill in evaluation which is also detailed in Chapter 14. Evaluation can occur throughout the essay, but at the very least, it must occur as a short paragraph, identifying the pros/cons with a statement that identifies where the data or proof seems to lie, prior to the conclusion. Evaluation demonstrates your mastery of a higher level thinking skill and through it, you demonstrate that you understand both the issues and the possible solution(s) to the real underlying problem posed by the question.

Conclude by summarizing the judgment or evaluation. The conclusion cannot be just a repetition of what you already said. It is a synthesis, a 'bringing together' of the thoughts and ideas you presented in your essay, but it does re-iterate or restate or summarize your thesis. **DO NOT** bring up new ideas, thoughts, concepts, or positions in this final paragraph.

Step 3. Apply the structure

While talking with a recently graduated student who is moving on to a professional career in Europe, I asked what academic support service at CSUB helped her the most. She said without a doubt it was the idea that there is a standard essay structure which can be applied across the spectrum of coursework.

Once she learned to apply the structure I share in this section, her anxiety associated with essays went away.

When you adopt this approach to essay (or research paper) writing, your anxiety diminishes. It is the anxiety that produces the pressure and stress, making relatively common, although not always simple, written assignments appear daunting, almost insurmountable, causing you to procrastinate. As you progress in your studies, you will be required to do many written assignments; some classes will require an essay for every class session. And, of course, almost every written exam has an essay component. The essay structure detailed in this chapter reduces the stress in your life by making every assignment similar and doable in nature. The tendency to procrastinate subsides because one essay is no more problematic than the other; the essays become an ordinary part of the university experience which are all attacked in the same way.

And as you write more essays using this structure, the process itself becomes easier. The process is consistent from essay to essay; while the content changes in those different courses, the structure is consistent regardless of your course discipline. The structure then paradoxically provides you with stress reducing assurance that any essay is possible at any time in any context. This freedom lets you focus on content while providing an essay, which is relatively easy for the professor to read, enhancing your scores.

The essay you write will be driven by a prompt by the teacher or by your own three-part question. Either way, when you adopt the following simple structure, your essay writing skills improve, your efficiency improves, and your life gets just a little bit easier. In the next section, I provide specific instruction and explanation on how to put the four or five-part structure into action for your essay.

The structure for writing your essay

Paragraph 1. You don't have to start P1 with the thesis sentence, but your thesis sentence must be in P1. In this first paragraph, you must include three or four sentences of support for this thesis. Each one of these sentences is identifying or describing a different point (or support for your thesis) and each sentence is then a 'map' of what you are going to talk about in the rest of your paper or essay. As you write your essay, remember to make/address the points in the same order as your thesis paragraph. If you don't mention it as a key point in your thesis paragraph, don't write about it later. (Or else, amend your thesis paragraph accordingly. This is why you make notes and a plan before starting to write).

Paragraph 2. In P2, you expand on, or explain, the first of the support sentences from P1. That sentence from P1 acts as the thesis of P2 (if you repeat it, change it slightly), followed by three to five sentences supporting your idea or point. So P2 should be about six sentences.

If it is paper that requires you to take a position, you will need to identify the pros and cons of each statement of support. Every solution to a problem has pros and cons, so you must identify them. Then, in the conclusion, you weigh all of the pros against all of the cons and see where the evidence 'weighs in.' You would do this again in subsequent paragraphs for each point you made in your thesis paragraph (P1). Generally, this is your strongest argument, the key point you want to make. Cite your sources of support. Explain why. And then make a transition to your next point, which is the thesis of P3.

Paragraph 3. This paragraph features the second of the support sentences from P1, which acts as the thesis of P3. This thesis sentence is then followed by three to five sentences of support or justification for that idea or point. As you can see, P3 is about six to 10 sentences in length and serves to support the second sentence of support you wrote in P1. You might identify the pro and con positions for each point of support or solution in this paragraph, which would add several sentences to the paragraph. In any case, cite your sources; for example, state that the professor said... or that the

PowerPoint included a reference to… or the textbook explained… Create a transition sentence into the next point.

Paragraph 4. This paragraph features the third support sentences from P1, which acts as the thesis of P4. This sentence is then followed by three to five sentences of support or justification for that idea or point. P4 is another six to 10 sentences. Further pro con analysis of this specific point, if needed, could add several more sentences. This is the third point of support you identified in paragraph one. Create a transition into your anecdotal support, if you have it.

Paragraph 5. This would be where you talk about your personal story, or identify the anecdotal evidence to support your position. This is what you think, based on what you have observed in day-to-day life. Since this is a story, use as many sentences as needed to tell your story. Then use a transition sentence to lead into your conclusion paragraph.

Paragraph 6. P6 is your Conclusion. You start with one or two sentences, which restate your thesis (don't just cut and paste your thesis statement from P1); it is a summary and/or evaluation of your ideas.

It is best to use this paragraph to place the issues and support in a wider context, but with continued emphasis upon the question. The conclusion is based on your analysis, not on cliché answers or opinions. It is here that you can bring in the diverse viewpoints enabled by the stakeholder model – *who* is affected and *how*.

This final paragraph might be relatively long if you still need to identify pro and con positions of the points you have made. If you are required to use the pro/con model, which will be determined by the question itself, you will have to weigh in here; do the 'pros' seem to outweigh the 'cons' or not?

You can end your paper with a statement which would seem to clinch your thesis; I think the best clincher is a story or 'anecdote' which tells the story and provides a picture of your answer, solution, or idea to the reader. P6 could be as few as three sentences or as many as 20, depending upon the depth.

Chapter 16

Example

As your coach, I have introduced the idea of a common essay structure and explained it in detail above. Now I will give you an example as a way to demonstrate what I am talking about. We are again going to use the question I used in explaining the benefit of a three-part question for your essay or paper; if the question from the professor is not an explicit three-part question like this, you still have to break it down into parts you can discuss in your essay.

Would non-monetary motivation methods reduce industrial relations problems while improving labor productivity at ABC Company?

[Comment: The first thing you have to do is figure out your answer to the question. Basically, it is a yes or no answer followed by discussion: will non-monetary motivational methods improve labor productivity AND reduce the industrial relations problems, or not. If you decide that non-monetary methods will solve the problem better than increased salaries or bonuses, you say yes and formulate your discussion around why that will be. If you decide that money or bonuses is better, you would answer no and formulate your discussion around why that is more likely. For the purposes of this demonstration, I will choose the affirmative response and create an essay structure, leaving out the details, but including the thesis, paragraph and transitions for each paragraph.]

Thesis P (P1)
[Comment: The thesis paragraph has a sentence with your answer and sentences for each key point you will discuss in subsequent paragraphs. These sentences, except your thesis/answer, are in the same order as your paragraphs will be in your paper. As you can see, the opening sentence (S1) identifies the two positions; therefore P2 is a basic discussion of monetary and non-monetary motivational methods and how each might appeal to the worker. The second sentence (S2) is your answer or thesis, and does not have its own paragraph. The third sentence (S3) talks about the problem, the generally accepted belief that money motivates, and what they hope will occur by the action; this sentence serves as the thesis sentence for P3. Sentence four (S4) identifies the concepts you are going to use to explain why monetary tools don't work in the long run and

provides a sampling of research supporting non-monetary motivational tools and how they each would work; P4 corresponds to this sentence. Sentence five is your conclusion, corresponding to P5].

P1 (S1) While many managers and workers think relatively low salary or lack of bonus potential is the primary reason for dissatisfaction in the workplace, research suggests that non-monetary motivational methods improve relations between workers and management as well as the relations amongst the workers better than money.

P1 (S2) Therefore, ABC company would be better served by focusing on non-monetary motivation tools to improve industrial relations while improving productivity

P1 (S3) The problem the company seeks to solve is a climate of declining industrial relations which is negatively affecting productivity and it needs to decide between money as a motivational tool or non-monetary motivational strategies.

P1 (S4) Based on HR research done by McGregor (Theory X/Theory Y) and Herzberg (Hygiene factors) applied to Maslow's Needs Hierarchy, non-monetary motivational methods will best solve the problem and improve productivity.

P1 (S5) ABC Company faces a problem that every company faces at some point in its life cycle and while some stay with the model of monetary rewards to motivate, most have found that research-based non-monetary motivational strategies work better to improve both industrial relations and productivity.

P2.

Indeed, many managers think that workers are dissatisfied in their job simply because of the salary. This only temporarily improves productivity, and any fundamental issues affecting climate are not addressed…[three to five more sentences talking about what motivation is, how it occurs, and how non-monetary motivation works]…This type of situation is not isolated to a few companies.

Chapter 16

P3.

In almost every company, friction exists between workers and management regarding pay and working conditions which affects morale and productivity and the response is often to focus on monetary rewards as a motivational tool...[You would then use several sentences to clarify the problem and why this is the case, especially when monetary motivation is used. Here you would talk about at least two common monetary tools, probably raises and bonuses paid when productivity metrics are matched. If you don't address the pros and cons of monetary motivation here, you would need to do it in the conclusion.] By focusing on money as a solution to the relationship between management and workers, management is inadvertently prolonging resolution of the problem.

P4.

While many companies continue to focus only on the theory of monetary motivation, research by Herzberg and McGregor suggests a better way to enhance industrial relations and improve productivity. ... [This is the key paragraph of your essay: discuss the nature of Herzberg's Hygiene factors and how an absence of money serves as a dissatisfier, and how more money does not make the worker satisfied and more productive. Also discuss Maslow's needs hierarchy and what McGregor discovered to be the key motivational factors for any worker. Finally, identify at least two strategies (flex time, worker-controlled office layout, project focus vs assembly line, etc., how they work and why they motivate.]...This leads me to conclude their best option is to utilize non-monetary motivational strategies.

P5.

Research suggests non-monetary motivational strategies are more effective than monetary motivational strategies in their endeavor to improve both relations and productivity...[Then you would summarize why, because... followed by an evaluative section in which you would write three to six sentences summarizing the pros and cons of using monetary strategies followed by three to six sentences about the pros and cons of both non-monetary strategies (if this has not already been done in the above paragraphs)...] In conclusion, it seems to me that the best strategy for ABC Company to use to solve their industrial relations problem while simultaneously improving performance is to use non-monetary motivational strategies and techniques.

Conclusion

This chapter concludes the specific strategies for improving your academic skill infrastructure. The next three chapters offer final thoughts on topics you have heard about before: time, academic honesty, and handling adversity.

What is different is that for each of these, I have written a chapter offering you specific strategies to help you deal with each issue you will inevitably need to handle in school. As with my previous chapters, I have moved beyond a general 'what' to do, which you have probably heard more than once, to a more specific 'how' to do it set of instructions.

Chapter 17
Time

Background Story.

A student came in, on time, for her 4:30 p.m. appointment with her academic support coach. She seated herself on the opposite side of my desk, both elbows on the desk, hands under her chin holding her head up. While retrieving her record on the computer, I heard a loud thunk; evidently, her head slipped from her hands and her head slammed face first onto the desktop. No blood and no black eyes, but she was in tears.

While you might think this humorous, the story is told not to amuse, but rather to exemplify time issues many students have to deal with. Obviously a student athlete, she had additional demands other students might not have to think about and because her sport was not fully funded she had to work a part time job. Clearly, she was very busy. As a swimmer she had: practice time in the pool, time with her strength and conditioning coach, time with her athletic trainer tending to injuries, time in class, time in study, time at work. She was simply exhausted by all of her school and work commitments and struggling to function day to day.

I suggested that instead of this study and tutoring appointment, perhaps it would be best if she just took a nap. She refused, saying she had to be at work at 5:30 p.m. and could not afford to be late or groggy. While athletes have many more time-consuming obligations than normal students, we have to understand that many other students also work to pay tuition and some have family obligations as well. This chapter is about how best to manage time.

Thoughts on Time

As exemplified by the above story, every student has time commitments. And sometimes these demands come at an exhausting price. So rather than attempting to endure a state of exhaustion in order to meet goals, you must first understand the nature of time, then create a structure which allows for the most efficient and effective use of the time available in order to meet those goals.

This is not to say you won't be tired, but sometimes the exhaustion is simply a side effect of mismanaged and misdirected effort in the time we are allotted.

The key for you to understand is that time is a currency for which there needs to be a spending plan. You are frequently told to budget your time; the question for many then becomes 'what exactly does that look like?'

Of the two components, the budget presumes you have finite time, just as you probably have finite money. To say you don't have enough time is inaccurate; we all have the same amount of time and the perception that we don't have enough is a function of how we use the time available to us (rather than the supply of time).

It helps for you have a calendar and to create a spreadsheet showing how you intend to allocate the time you have. To do this best, it would help you to first write down how you are currently spending your time. This raw data provides you with a reality that you can then adjust to meet your needs, or confront, as the case might be.

Once you have the record showing where you are, in fact, spending your time, you can then create a spending plan, which would be your intentions of where the time needs to be allocated. The budget would be the time allocation for each obligation, which you enter into the calendar and/or spreadsheet to help provide some self-accountability; indeed, a budget at least sounds more restrictive than a spending plan.

To create the spending plan of your time, you start with the essentials, the non-negotiables. These would be demands on your time from school and team, including everything I mentioned in the story opening this chapter. Then move to family, work, and personal time. Social time is important, but consider how much time is already going into the myriad of social activities on your phone, which is basically a #timeblackhole.

While everyone has the same amount of time available, not all students are created equally when it comes where you spend that time. Students without athletic commitments, or students who are not trying to juggle a job with a school schedule and a family at home, might not realize how much time they are spending in frivolous ways. Conversely, student athletes must realize they simply cannot spend their time the same way these more carefree students seem to.

Every university introductory course designed to help students develop the skills needed to be successful at that school invariably tells the student what they need to do. This includes the need to manage their time. When I was assisting our Athletic Director teach this course at CSUB, I heard him tell students things like 'manage your time' or 'work hard' in response to which most students shook their heads earnestly, showing that they seemed to get it, although some rolled their eyes, mostly because they had heard advice like that hundreds of times. In spite of this repeated recommendation to manage time, many students still waste time, spending it in inefficient or ineffective ways.

What is time management? Why do you need to efficiently manage time? Because time is a resource that is scarce. While a song by the Rolling Stones from the 60s said 'time is on my side' – it is not.

Society divides time into organizable chunks based on the earth's position relative to the sun. And basically you need some sleep, generally at night, in order to survive, so you are left with a cycle of 16 hours or so, in every 24-hour period, to accomplish the things you need to get done.

Everyone is in this same cycle because everyone has the same 24-hour cycle available. *You simply cannot excuse yourself by saying you don't have enough time!*

How to Maximize your Time

The first step in the efficient management of available time is some sort of calendar that you can update every time an activity, assignment, deadline, or exam is announced.

Some students like the little notebook agenda calendar, which many schools provide for their students. Others like to use Google calendar or a something similar. When I was coaching, all of the basketball players were grouped into Google calendar, but some did not take the time to update it based on their academic needs, thinking it applied only to their athletic lives. It should apply to everything.

Why is a calendar important? It enables you to have a daily routine. As you go to bed, you look at it to become aware of your next day's activity. As you wake up in the morning, it's what you look at first; you have a clear mental picture of what your day looks like. It also enhances your study routine, as it provides guidance as to the purpose of the time you are going to spend in your BC/AC routines.

Separate to time management, you need to organize your academic materials. In addition to study using three decks/boxes of color-coded flashcards, I recommend that you have one wirebound notebook for EACH class in which you will take your notes. I like to use the quadrille graphing paper notebooks for notes because it is easier to draw graphs and charts as well keep notes aligned. In addition, you need a three-ring binder or folder for EACH class in which you will put EVERY piece of paper your professor gives you.

Next, differentiate the types of time commitments you have. Most students have three chunks of time they have to manage:

1. class and study

2. social/recreation

3. eat/sleep

Some students have to manage a fourth chunk of time necessitated by a job, or work study, or varsity athletics. Some more students have a fifth chunk of time to manage, necessitated by attending to the needs of their family.

The key to academic success is to treat the academic part of your life like a second job, for which you will need to regularly schedule activities. While going to class is important, success requires more than that.

Summary of the BC/DC/AC Study Sequence Process

Assume a Monday-Wednesday-Friday class sequence for this example:

BC/Before. For Monday's class, on Saturday or Sunday, do the pre-class preparation, which is the quick read, creating the flash cards with terminology from the chapter and the professor's lecture.

DC/During Monday's class, be sure to get to class on time, sit in the front, turn off electronics (do not take notes on your phone/laptop/notebook), take earbuds out, your hat off, and your sunglasses off. Take notes in your class-specific notebook using the Cornell method I reviewed in Chapter 8.

AC/After class on Monday, *right after class*, spend 10 minutes reviewing your notes as instructed.

AC/After Monday's class, on Tuesday go to your predesignated place at a predetermined and regular time and spend about 90 minutes doing the following: a 10 minute notes review, a 10 minute recall/self quiz with note cards, 20 minutes doing at least three problems at the end of the chapter, then spend about an hour (in 20 minute intervals) to read the chapter completely through in one sitting circling terms/concepts you still don't get.

BC/Before Wednesday's class, at some point on Tuesday after the above AC routine, spend about an hour in preparation for Wednesday's lecture. Review the pre-class routine.

DC/During class Wednesday follow your DC routine.

AC/After class Wednesday, *immediately after class*, do your 10 minute review. Then sometime Wednesday, spend an additional 20 minutes doing flash card recall using box/deck 2 of your flashcards.

AC/After Wednesday's class, sometime on Thursday, you need to devote about 90 minutes to a study session during which you will spend 10 minutes on your notes review, 20 minutes on recall with the flashcard self quiz of cards in box/deck 1, 20 minutes working at least three problems at the end of the chapter, and about an hour reading the chapter completely through in 20 minute intervals, circling the items you still don't get.

BC/Before Friday's class, spend about an hour on Thursday doing the prep for Friday's class session. Then do another 10 minute review from the Wednesday lecture.

DC/During class on Friday, do your DC routine.

AC/After class on Friday spend 10 minutes on your notes as soon as class is over.

AC/Saturday do the AC routine for Friday's class during which you will spend up to 90 minutes on the four steps in the AC/After Class routine for the last classes attended. Then spend an hour doing your BC routine for each of Monday's class(es).

AC/BC Sunday. Spend 20 minutes doing the flashcard self quiz on cards in box/deck 3 and another 20 minutes doing the flashcard self quiz from box 1. Then spend another three hours working on any papers, reports, or homework assignments. If the course is designed so that you don't have text to read and instead have problems to do, (such as you might find in a science, math, or accounting class) you can use that last hour of your Sunday session to do that work instead of the reading.

The above example is for one class over one week. Repeat the cycle for each class. If you are taking three lecture classes, you will need to do this three separate times. As you can see, being a student requires more time OUT of class than in class. Remember, the time spent for self quiz/review with the flashcards involves ALL classes so you don't spend an hour with flash cards for each class every day. Just do the flash card centered self quiz in 20 minute blocks of time whenever and wherever the opportunity presents itself as long as you get through your deck of 'don't know' cards at least once a day.

By embracing this BC/DC/AC routine, including the flashcard self quizzes, you will see or hear or read material several times. It is this process of recall that enables you to embed the information into your memory. Looking at it once does not work for most people.

By using this process, you will see, hear, read, or recall the terminology and information you need to know at least 10 times before your first quiz/exam. Utilizing this strategy significantly increases the number of times you will see the material, not to mention the number of times you quiz yourself about it, greatly improving your retention, knowledge, and comprehension. The more you see and recall it, the more embedded it becomes. The following quick review enables you to see, hear, and review the terms/concepts at least 15 times before the final.

Quick BC/DC/AC Routine Review

1. Try to get the PowerPoint before class

2. Quick read assigned chapter

3. Define terms; create flash cards

4. Observe the PowerPoint in class and listen to the lecture

5. Take notes

6. 10 minute review of notes the same day

7. 10 minute review of notes the next day

8. Box/deck 1 flash card self quiz daily (all classes)

9. Read the chapter in its entirety in one sitting, after quick read, but no later than next day

10. Answer at least three questions from the end of chapter review/summary

11. Box/deck 1 flash card self quiz the next day; do every day

12. Box/deck 2 flash card self quiz every three days

13. Once a week, 10 minute note review for each day of class that week

14. Once a week, box/deck 3 flash card self quiz

15. Final exam review questions and any class-driven study sessions for that final

How will you spend your time? Here is a sample spending plan to help you to organize your own plan.

Monday-Friday. Every day, plan on spending time similar to this:

- 1.5 hrs - Eat well; 30 minutes each meal

- 8 hrs - Sleep; 8 hrs from 11 p.m. to 7 a.m. is better

- 3 hrs - BC Routines or AC routines (depends on day)

- 3 hrs - Class (3 classes, but depends on day)

- 4 hrs - Job or varsity sport

Chapter 17

- 0.5 hr - Self quiz; flashcard box/deck 1 and/or 2
- 2 hrs - Do end of chapter problems or group study
- 1 hr - Open
- 1 hr - Travel to and from locations

Saturday

- 1.5 hrs - Eat
- 8 hrs - Sleep
- 4 hrs - Job or varsity sport
- 0.5 hr - Flash cards box/deck 1
- 3 hrs - BC routines for Monday's classes [could be done Sunday]
- 3 hrs - AC routine for Friday's classes
- 4 hrs - Recreation, shopping, laundry, bills

Sunday

- 1.5 hrs - Eat
- 8 hrs - Sleep
- 8.5 hrs (or 5.5 hrs) - Social, relax
- 1 hr - Flashcard box/deck 1 & 3
- 3 hrs (or 6 hrs) - Dedicated study to catch up, work on research, do classroom assignments not yet complete; do this in 50 minute segments with 10 minute break between each segment.

If you skip the BC routine on Saturday, you would need to do it on Sunday, making for a very long study day.

Conclusion

As you can see, a plan for spending your time is a guide for your intentions and will vary from person to person. A spending plan should not be seen as a restriction, but rather as a way to more efficiently take advantage of the time available to you. Of course, your family situation might require that time be allocated in a different way. Or your coach might organize your day slightly differently.

Any which way you look at it, being a student requires time to be spent doing the BC/DC/AC routines, all of which are necessary steps in your learning progression. As I said earlier, there is no shortcut, but once you are organized and have a spending plan in mind, you will experience less anxiety. And as you become better at your routines, the time needed for those will likely diminish as well.

In the next chapter, I talk about academic integrity, which has become one of the most-discussed educational topics in post-secondary education. Stories about academic malpractice appear every few weeks in the press. This has created an urgent discussion among academic advisors, professors, coaches, and college administrators who are striving to maintain the purpose and mission of higher education while challenging this evidently growing tendency by students to cheat.

Regardless of what is going on around you, inside and outside school, it is crucial for your own development to do your own work and avoid anything that might be considered academic malpractice. Why and how to do this is the focus of Chapter 18.

Chapter 18
Embrace Academic
Integrity

There is no shortcut: To become smarter, do your own work. When you don't, you cripple yourself.

In the early 1990s, I was a presenter at a series of conference workshops sponsored by the Drug Enforcement Agency and the National High School Coaches Association.

As athletic director at Aspen High School, I had written a 10-hour drug education course and accompanying text for student athletes who had violated the code of conduct after pledging to follow the policy of the school. This relatively progressive idea, which I called *Developing the Discrepancy of Substance Use by Students and Athletes,* was then presented to coaches and athletic directors as a way to enhance drug prevention efforts in their athletic programs and for their student-athletes.

At a conference in Tucson, Arizona, I had the opportunity to present on the same program with Dr. Tom Tutko of San Jose State University, at the time the leader in sport psychology. We spent time at lunch talking about my idea and his seminal 1976 book, *Sports Psyching.* During our conversation, he touched on the idea that student athletes and coaches focus too much on the results, on the win, which then encourages them to cheat. Of course, the cheating in this case was in the form of performance enhancing drugs. He argued that instead of a focus on the score, on the win, on the results, both athletes and coaches should focus on the process, working to incrementally improve.

The challenge in athletics, of course, is keeping everyone on the same page; game theory is in play with performance enhancing drugs. If one person cheats, and does not get caught, the rewards can be significant, often more than the potential downside, so there is a serious incentive to cheat. Just check out Lance Armstrong's unprecedented seven wins on the Tour de France taking him to superstar status and top 10% income level. We were amazed by the superhuman effort of someone coming off chemo treatment enabling him to recover from cancer, thinking no person could possibly ride like that for three weeks. Evidently, we were right!

What I inferred from my conversation with Tom Tutko was that this focus on result could also encourage the same student athlete to cheat in the classroom. I began to wonder if the occasional academic scandals by student athletes at the university level were simply a symptom of this focus on results, and a need to get ahead with some sort of unauthorized assistance. Indeed, sport psychologist Shane Murphy wrote a book in 1996 called *The Achievement Zone* in which he argued that results-focused athletes see only short term success and are happy only when basking in that success. But he argued that this results-focused model has drawbacks and cannot lead to long term success; the biggest shortcoming of the results-only model "is that people will sometimes break the rules to maintain their highly successful image." In other words, they will cheat to win, or to get that acceptable grade. And as I surmised above, if everyone really does cheat, then the diploma or grade is virtually worthless because value in that college education comes from the challenge, the effort, the rigor. If everyone is able to get that same result through cheating, then no one has a competitive advantage; the diploma has to be replaced by some other qualification of achievement.

In the end, a focus on process, or what Murphy calls the action focus, is the only way to keep improving and to see consistent positive results. And according to Murphy, this action focus can be learned. The Academic Weight Room is a way to keep an action focus to strengthen your academic skill set without resorting to cheating.

What is Academic Integrity?

Academic integrity is related to credibility; credibility is doing what you said you would do. Students who demonstrate academic integrity can be trusted, which is a characteristic that will serve each student well upon matriculation and movement into a career pathway.

The corollary of academic integrity is academic malpractice. Malpractice from a legal standpoint is a form of negligence. A professional (doctor, lawyer, dentist, teacher, coach) or business has a *duty* to make sure the patient, client, student, athlete, or customer is not injured when doing what the professional says, or when using a product in the way the company has designed.

Whilst a student does not have the same duty to a school or professor as the school or professor has to the student – a duty of sorts is still established when the student is admitted to the school and agrees to adhere to the policies governing academic integrity. Academic malpractice then occurs when a student says they will follow the rules and do their own work but instead does something contrary to what they said. This discrepancy calls into question the student's credibility and integrity.

The school/university and athletic department, either explicitly or implicitly, almost always requires that you adhere to an honor code in your academic work which requires you to do your own work. By attending the school and participating in the program, which you have *chosen* to do, you either explicitly or implicitly agree to practice academic integrity, or refrain from academic malpractice. Virtually every professor includes on his/her syllabus significant information and/or warning about academic integrity and what will happen to you if you are dishonest in your academic endeavors in that class.

At Bakersfield, the faculty have adopted an Academic Honesty policy, which all faculty are expected to enforce. Taken from the CSUB course of study: "The principles of truth and integrity are recognized as fundamental to a community of teachers and scholars. The University expects that both faculty and student will honor these principles and in so doing will protect the integrity of all academic work and student grades. Students are expected to do all work assigned to them without unauthorized assistance and without giving unauthorized assistance. Academic dishonesty is a broad category of actions that involved fraud and deception to improve a grade or obtain course credit. Academic dishonesty (cheating) is not limited to examination situations alone, but arises whenever students attempt to gain an unearned academic advantage."

Not Everyone Cheats

More than once, I have heard students justify questionable behavior by citing the actions of others. I am told to look at the investment bankers who drove our economy into the tank. Or look at the juicers in baseball who hit all those home runs. Or look at professional cyclists like Lance Armstrong who evidently cheated to win millions of dollars in prize money and endorsements. Or even nationally recognized universities that created fake classes for which students got credit for writing one paper.

All of those examples identify cases where cheating occurred. But just because it happened does not mean it is right, nor does it mean you should also cheat to get ahead. Even if it seems that everyone is doing it, the reality is that not everyone is. The movie *Old School* has a scene where Frank the Tank, played by Will Ferrell, gets drunk at a fraternity party and proceeds to lead the other partygoers streaking, naked, down the street. When his wife and her friends coincidentally happen by in her car, she rolls down her window and asks Frank what he's doing. He replies, "We're streaking, honey." "Who's streaking?" she asks. Frank replies, "Everyone's doing it." Of course, nobody else is streaking. The moral to that embarrassingly funny, totally absurd episode is that while it seems like a good idea at the time, and while it looks like everyone is at the party (or in on the cheating), there is a pretty good chance that most students are trying to do the right thing. And in school, most students accept the rigor and realize there are no shortcuts. They maintain their academic integrity, enhance their own credibility, and ensure that the results are a function of their own effort rather than the effort of others.

Even if you try to excuse academic malpractice by ignoring, or pretending NOT to notice policies requiring academic integrity, and even if you try to excuse it by saying that everyone is doing it, cheating is wrong and is detrimental to your own educational process.

What Does Academic Malpractice Look Like?

There are a variety of behaviors that are considered dishonest in an academic setting. Because so many students seem to have no problem seeking the easiest, fastest way to a good grade, it might be best to refer to your own school's handbook for a full description of all behaviors which constitute academic malpractice.

Plagiarism is probably the most pervasive form of cheating, but it is just one type of academic dishonesty. The practice of taking someone else's work or ideas and passing them off as one's own, plagiarism includes the strategy of copy-and-paste from documents, articles, or other papers found via Google or Wikipedia, or using another's ideas without attribution. It also includes submitting work that someone else has completed or done for you, or using work that someone else previously submitted for your class or another class. This would include submitting your OWN paper in two or more different classes, even a year or two later, without receiving the professor's prior approval before doing so.

It is simply too easy for the professor to figure out if you are utilizing a copy-and-paste technique to complete a paper, or using a paper which you (or someone else) submitted last year for the same (or even a different) course.

There is not much hope for you if you do get caught cheating in this way. The evidence is always strong as most documents are submitted electronically as well as in hard copy and regardless of what you think, it is relatively easy for them to figure out or even see exactly where you have cheated. Online paper checking services such as Turnitin.com or others are generally utilized by most professors, so once your document is submitted electronically it is almost always checked against everything else submitted to the web. In other words, your paper is compared with millions of other documents for similarities and plagiarism.

One of the easiest places to cheat is during online courses, or during online quizzes for a traditional or hybrid course. When you are expected to complete an online course, you can demonstrate and/or practice academic integrity by engaging in the following activities and suggestions.

- Read any and all applicable assignments and material prior to starting the quiz.

- Do not wait until the last possible minute to take the quiz.

- Work independently; do not attempt a quiz as a group or with another person in the class.

- If it is an open book quiz, find your own answer from the readings or the text; do not ask those around you for the answer.

- Do not copy-and-paste an answer from another source or student.

- Do not ask another student for an answer or document you need for an answer.

- Do not give an answer or a document to another student.

- Don't refresh the page.

- Don't 'go back' to see something you have previously completed.

If something happens beyond your control which causes you to be 'locked out' of an online quiz, let one of the academic support advisors know so she/he can email your professor to ask for a re-start. For example, there are cases when laptops shut down because laptop batteries have run out and the computer is not plugged in. Check batteries before starting and understand all the protocols of the particular quiz before starting.

Understand that an occasional restart might be necessary but do not expect you will be able to do this on a regular basis, if at all. Restarts are a courtesy afforded by the professor and are not to be taken lightly. Some professors will not give you the benefit of the doubt while others will. All professors will call you out if there is a pattern of abuse detected and you will be very fortunate indeed to stay in school when that happens. It is best to just do what you are supposed to do.

How do you maintain academic integrity?

Basically, you do what you are supposed to do! If we all simply did what we are supposed to do, in the classroom, in the gym, on the road, at home, everything would move so much more smoothly for all.

Of course, doing what you are supposed to do is not necessarily the easiest thing, but it is the way to more robust and enduring results. A student who does his/her own work is embracing academic integrity. A student who embraces the process of incremental academic improvement by strengthening their academic skill set (rather than seeking the easy way out offered through cheating) is maintaining academic integrity. Essentially, it is as easy (and hard) as doing your own work, striving to put strategies of study skills, essay skills, and examinations tactics into play, and engaging in the difficult job of knowledge acquisition.

Why Embrace Academic Integrity?

While it is easier to cheat than to embrace and accept the rigor of education, the credibility of your own performance is compromised and the value of everyone else's diploma is diminished when you cheat. More importantly, you are not just cheating the university and the system, you are cheating yourself. When you KNOW you did not do the work, you will then realize that you have missed the whole point of higher education.

It is crippling to cheat, even if the grade or score makes you feel pretty good for a minute. When you know someone else is the reason for your success, you will have a lack of confidence in your own abilities which will cripple your competitive advantage when it comes to a job. You do not want to be that person who shies away from the challenge. That person who is not sure he/she can actually do what might need to be done. That deer in the headlights, frozen in time as the vehicle of a good job bears down. You don't want to be, Peter Gabriel's words, "hovering like a fly, waiting for the windshield on the freeway." But that is a possibility if you succumb to academic malpractice to get results without the requisite work.

Chapter 18

Conclusion

The current situation at the postsecondary level is one of scrutiny. Almost everyone I talk to is expressing concern about academic honesty, especially with respect to online courses. But the concern is not limited to that model. There are plenty of reasons for educators and parents to be concerned about academic integrity in education in general, and what seems to be the little or no concern shown by current students about the problem.

While we focused on academic integrity in this chapter, one reason for the need to cheat is the expectation that you must win, or excel, in whatever you do. This focus on the need to win has created a surreal environment for both students and athletes. The pressure to succeed is universal; society loves a winner. That's why I spend the next chapter talking about success, and the need to understand that winning is different from success and losing is different from failure.

It is important to understand the nature of success and what you can do to actually succeed. However, it might be more important to learn what to do when things don't go your way. It is our fear of losing, our fear of failing, our fear of setbacks that leads us to cheat, whether that is by using performance-enhancing substances in athletics or committing academic malpractice in the classroom.

Chapter 19
How to be More
Successful

"Success is always a process, never an event. Failure is always an event, never a person." Manolis Votsis.

Neal Beidleman, a former student at Aspen High School and member of the track team I coached during my first years as a teacher/coach went on to become an aerospace engineer but his passion was mountain climbing and it is this passion which connected him with one of the great tragedies on Mount Everest. This is the story he shared about that experience during an annual senior athlete banquet at AHS sometime between 2005 and 2007.

In 1996, Beidleman was a professional climbing guide hired to help a group of aspiring climbers, led by the renowned Scott Fischer, summit Mount Everest. It is during a very small window of opportunity in May that the weather patterns generally enable hundreds of mountain climbers to attempt one of the most difficult mountain ascents in the world. Several different expeditions gathered to attempt their ascents, creating a veritable traffic jam of climbers on that day. But their seemingly normal, yet challenging and dangerous climb spiraled into a disaster for a variety of reasons.

Into Thin Air by Jon Krakauer, and *The Climb* by Anatoli Boukreev, both written shortly after the historic events unfolded, are accounts which address the tragedy from different perspectives. Boukreev was a guide on Fischer's team and was able to provide a first-hand description, while Krakauer covered tragedy from the perspective of an outside investigative reporter. Both books are compelling, and each find faults in different places.

The tragedy unfolded when a perfect storm of events culminated in the deaths of eight climbers. First, the climbers were surprised by an unusual and unforeseen storm which engulfed them while they were far above their camp. Secondly, each of the lead guides were almost forced by their paying customers to get them to the top, making a forced push to the summit well after the previously agreed upon turnaround time had passed; after all, these customers had paid thousands of dollars to summit Everest and they were oh-so-close. And because they did not turn around at the previously agreed-upon time, they put themselves into a dangerous position, even without the fast closing storm. Through poor visibility coupled with exhaustion and oxygen deficit of the amateur climbers, each of these lead guides lost track of their own groups as they dealt with the few who demanded to go on up.

On his own way down Neal happened across a group of disoriented and struggling climbers belonging to a different guide who had lost their way. He gathered them up and led them down the 'trail' in the raging blizzard. Eventually, they came to a col, or a flat spot on the mountain, which is also where he knew their base camp would be located. But unable see anything in the hurricane force winds and driving snow, he was not sure where they were on that col. He did know that going the wrong way would result in certain death as one edge of the col dropped off into 1,000 feet of emptiness. Because of that uncertainty and group disorientation, exacerbated by the lack of oxygen, he had the group huddle up and hunker down in the deadly-cold storm to regroup while he tried to figure out the best way to the safety of the base camp.

Grasping the opportunity presented by the momentary clear sky of the eye of the storm, he was able to catch a glimpse of enough of the night sky to orient himself using the stars as guidance (a skill he learned in science class and enhanced during our experiential education program at Aspen High School). Calculating his likely location based on what he saw of the stars, he figured the camp was to his left, he then told everyone they needed to gather themselves together and make their way, following his steps. One was struggling and indicated that Neal should go on. Another said she couldn't make it without being carried; he yelled above the howling storm that if he tried to carry her, they would both die. He had no choice but to move forward with the three who could make their own way. He left without her. Another climber whom he left eventually, miraculously, found his way to the base camp on his own.

Neal told our group how the truth of the story is sad, ugly, and brutal, one he does not like to talk about and one for which he wants no heroic recognition. He said everyone had a positive expectation of summiting Everest, yet some did not make it home. While he saved lives as he used his skill to lead them down the mountain, the fact that some died has created a burden, an adversity to overcome. The entire story of the Everest tragedy of 1996 is told in the movie *Everest*.

What can We Learn from his Story?

I shared this story during a presentation to the men's basketball team at Georgia State. Their first reaction was disbelief, mostly because none of the players would even think of doing anything remotely connected to the snow, let alone in the sub-zero conditions of Everest, so it was tough to get them to see what I was trying to accomplish. At first, they were seeing things too literally. Eventually, I got them to look past the mountain climbing as an activity that didn't relate to them at all, to consider the story as source material for a case study in leadership and handling adversity.

Clearly Neal was put into a difficult place when human frailty collided with nature, but it was his skill on the mountain and as a leader which enabled him, along with most of the climbers he was with, to successfully navigate to the base camp. His mountaineering skills were nurtured in the challenging hikes and climbs of his surroundings, but his technical skills were further developed via a purposeful and specific outdoor education course in the Aspen schools. It teaches students how to be self-sufficient in the outdoors, beginning in the elementary grades and progressing in difficulty and challenge through grade 12, including a rigorous weeklong outdoor education experience in grade 8.

Of course, my focus with the team was not the nature of the mountains, including rocky trails, steep inclines, quickly changing conditions, cold temperatures, strong winds, and lack of oxygen, but rather Neal's planning and preparation for the ascent, which actually took years and were without reproach, and then what he did when confronted with such incredible adversity. His story gave me a chance to talk with the players about winning and losing, success and failure, common traits of successful people, leadership, and how to handle adversity. The intangible skills which enabled his success on Everest can be learned by anyone and put into practice when the situation requires. Legendary UCLA basketball coach John Wooden, in his Pyramid of Success, defines skill as "the knowledge of and the ability to properly and quickly execute" an action, achieved through practice and preparation, which Neal exemplified.

Indeed, success for Neal and his rescued climbers was a function of experience, preparation, mental toughness, and an ability to bring a laser-like focus to the present situation. Utilizing discipline and patience, he understood it was necessary to approach the situation one step at time; they neared the summit one excruciatingly painful step at a time and he knew the trip back down was necessarily one step at a time. Either way, he knew he could not hurry. (Strive for quickness, but do not hurry.) For Neal, any haste in his descent or decision-making process at the col could easily have resulted in poor decisions.

The idea that the only reality is what is happening at this exact moment is the guiding principle of the burgeoning mindfulness movement. I doubt Neal was taught to be mindful out of that program but it is clear he was able to focus on the moment, controlling the likely inevitable negative thoughts and the multitude of distractions that interfered with his most immediate concern: survival. Many, perhaps most, would crumble under that onslaught of adverse conditions. In spite of the many negative factors putting their very survival in doubt, Neal demonstrated a toughness which enabled him to transcend. Had Neal paid attention to any of the negative distractions, it is likely he would not have enough brain power to get to the solution to the problem they faced.

Jim Thompson, who founded Positive Coaching Alliance, spoke about this when he presented to coaches and parents of Aspen HS during my tenure as athletic director. Without getting into the details of his entire philosophy, he argues that how a coach and/or parent treats an athlete after a mistake (or loss) will affect their anxiety levels in subsequent efforts; negative coaching or parenting which is critical of the erring athlete results in anxiety and poor results while positive coaching and parenting results in less anxiety and better results. When you don't worry about failing, when you feel in control of your actions, you have the necessary energy to accomplish the task in front of you. Again, I don't think Neal was a beneficiary of this coaching philosophy, but he does provide an example of what happens when you are able to control anxiety through a mindful ability to focus.

While it is not likely you will experience any adversity that matches the severity which Beidleman's story exemplifies, everyone has challenges to deal with. A poor grade is a form of adversity, as is a difficult examination in the classroom, a difficult term schedule, a notoriously tough professor for the term, fatigue, or illness; the severity of adversity increases as the list of challenges grows.

A key characteristic of a successful student is the ability to handle adversity, which is related to toughness and grit, a similar trait which has received a lot of coverage. When dealing with the possibility of adversity, one strategy is to simply avoid any possibility of failure, to attempt only the things that are clearly 'winnable;' of course, that pretty much eliminates most competitive or challenging endeavors. Since avoidance is impossible for just about everyone, there are several skills and characteristics we can adopt to better deal with the inevitable. To accomplish this, you must begin to formulate your own definition of success; to that end I will offer a discussion of my own discovery process.

On Success and Failure

From the beginning of my coaching and teaching career, I scuffled with my own definition of success and the accompanying idea of failure. Of course, I wanted to win, and we won often. But we also lost. Soon, it became clear that no matter what I did as a coach, some days we simply did not have enough talent to score more points or run faster. So, were we then failures because we did not win? It did not take long for me to realize that winning was not necessarily success (despite societal demands to the contrary), that success was temporary, that losing was not failure, and that failure was not fatal.

It was at this point I realized that the process was more important in the long run than the immediate result; the focus on results created anxiety which negatively affected our performance. Once we focused on the process of becoming better, our performance improved and the score took care of itself. Moving students from the mindset which equated a win with success to a mindset where everyone saw growth (as a result of either a win or loss) as success became one of my most important actions as coach. I had to teach many students about the desirability of the growth mindset in the process of becoming a better student or player.

The lessons of Neal's experience on Everest confirm my belief that if you plan and prepare diligently, if you study and practice with purpose, if you are 'here, now,' if you focus on what needs to be done in the moment rather than worrying about what just happened or what might happen in the future, you are doing what you reasonably can to be successful. You have done what is necessary to put yourself in a position to win. A negative outcome is a failed attempt rather than failure.

The very nature of a competitive event in which a score is kept, generally sees at least one of the teams or participants lose. In most situations, half of all teams who have played games in the past week will lose. In many competitions, like running or bicycling races or chess tournaments, only one person wins. In your own endeavor, you might win and you might not win; what is most important in that process is that you strived to win. Then, whether you win or lose, you continue to pursue growth and improvement. And I recommend you stay away from measuring your success by wins or how well you do against someone else, even the one who beat you. You might have lost, but if you performed at a level superior than any previous attempt, you can't consider that loss a failure. Success should be measured against yourself while winning is measured against someone else. The key point to remember in this is that only you can define the metric which defines your own success.

The same holds true in the classroom, which is just a slightly different type of competitive environment. Because you have chosen to pursue higher education, it makes sense to apply the skills discussed in this book to guide your best effort. Your grade is simply an estimate by the professor of the progress of your attainment of the content, your comprehension of the concepts. This grade shows how you fared compared to the rubric the professor had established to measure the attainment of those goals and objectives. The grade marks your level of progress in that process; it is a temporary marker that tells you more about what you don't know than what you do know and this enables you to figure out a better strategy, routine, or technique to gain that knowledge. It is simply growth vs outcome. If you embrace the process, and use the interim reports to guide your progress, results will improve. To provide additional insight into this success/failure discussion, I have included a few thoughts from other writers.

A journalist for *The Guardian* newspaper, Tom Lamont, wrote an article discussing the concept of success and failure for Olympic athletes; indeed, he questions how an Olympic athlete could possibly be unsuccessful. In *My Big Fail: Losers Come Clean on their All-Time Low*, Lamont identifies the bilateral nature of success and failure: because we are striving for success, we also have to be willing to encounter and deal with failure.

One of the people he interviews is Andrew Keller, head of the advertising agency which put together the advertising campaign which rescued Domino's Pizza. In the story, Keller says "Culture rewards success. That's what humanity is all about, survival of the fittest. And that's what we're rewarded for, by our parents, by our schools, and by government. There aren't many social endorsements of failure; you don't have shelves full of trophies that celebrate failure. So failure becomes taboo." But in recognition of the inevitability of failure and our need to deal with it, Lamont quotes Andrew Keller saying to his children "The reality is that failure is going to happen to all of us. It is going to happen to you."

This article introduced to me a small book of poetry by Pulitzer Prize winner Philip Schultz. His book *Failure* included the sad story of an almost impossible string of failed endeavors by his father, which he wrote to help others recognize that while his father might have been a failure, he was somebody who tried, who lived, who was always looking to get a win on his next effort. Schultz says that, "success and failure are almost artificial. People fall into the way of thinking that there's one or the other, it's black or white, that there's no in between. Of course, we all live in between."

Whatever your working definition of success becomes, know that success does not come easily, fairly, equally, or automatically to everyone. You must put the work in to give yourself a chance.

Chance implies something other than talent and effort is in play in the results of your endeavors. I have heard leadership experts say success is a function of hard work and talent, and any luck is simply when that combination meets opportunity. Still, it is important to at least acknowledge that simple random chance, or luck, has at least something to do with what we call success. Scott Adams says, "All success is luck, if you track it back to its source. The largest component of success is timing. When the universe and I have been on a compatible schedule, entirely by chance, things have worked out swimmingly. When my timing has been off, no amount of hard work or talent has mattered."

Nassim Taleb says in his book *Fooled by Randomness* that much of what we see as success is simply random events aligning to make it look like someone is smart. The world is full of wealthy people who were simply in the right place at the right time, or the right place at the wrong time, or the wrong place at the wrong time. The point is that more often than not, successful people identify their own intelligence or initiative as the cause for their success, but discount failures as 'bad luck.' Of course, you can't have it both ways; the randomness affects us both positively and negatively.

Adams argues that this randomness is not necessarily luck, but rather the outcomes of probabilities. "You can't directly control luck, but you can move from a game with low odds of success to a game with better odds." In my statistics course at university, the professor talked about the probability of a coin flip as 50-50 heads/tails. If we had a tournament of coin flips, with all heads continuing to the next round, every time there was a flip of the coin, there was a 50-50 chance of heads and when the final winner was crowned, it was not a matter of skill or luck, but rather probability. She/he simply was on the 'winning' side of the 50-50 flip. The winner was not 'lucky.' Random probability was in play, no more no less. Adams argues that odds matter and we need to "learn how to see patterns and determine odds within our actions and options."

To be successful we must learn to avoid low percentage plays evidenced by observation and analysis of the data. Again, when looking at the Everest example, it is easy to see in hindsight that the two lead guides eschewed the safer alternative when they went against the data-driven and observation-based rule to turn around at a certain time, no matter what. In order to appease clients, they instead chose to continue to the top, a decision which collided with the bad luck or bad timing of the superstorm they encountered on the way down.

Still, there is an aphorism which holds much truth: Luck is when opportunity meets preparation. Adams is the founder and artist of the popular comic strip Dilbert, of which he says its success, "is mostly a story of luck. I did make it easier for luck to find me and I was thoroughly prepared when it did." However, if you "believe all success is luck, you are not likely to try as hard as if you believe success comes from hard work… history tells us you still need to work hard to pull it off. Luck won't give you a strategy or system, you have to do that yourself."

To conclude this exploration of success and failure, Adams offers this: "Failure is where success likes to hide in plain sight." The next section helps you get to that success.

How to be successful

According to Vernacchia et al, in their book *Coaching Mental Excellence*, success is a function of four factors: ability, preparation, effort, and will. Everyone has ability, which is an acquired or natural capacity or talent that enables an individual to perform a particular job or task. You have ability in both academics and athletics or you would not be here. Ability is basically the same as talent. Study any successful athlete and you will find that ability is important, but they did not achieve on ability alone. It took preparation combined with effort, often more effort than they thought they could exert. But to make it all happen to the level for which they are recognized required more; the will the authors talk about is an internal strength, a tenacity, an ability to draw upon a personal reservoir of strength, stamina, confidence, composure, and 'guts' to get through tough starts, formidable opponents, and tight finishes.

As I mentioned in the section on academic integrity, I spent time with Dr. Tom Tutko when I was a presenter at drug abuse prevention seminars sponsored by NHSCA and DEA. Tutko is considered the founding father of sport psychology and I was indeed privileged to be part of casual conversations during which he commented on both athletic and academic performance by students and what coaches, teachers, and parents can do to enhance the student-athlete's success. While much of the discussion was about the detrimental effects of performance enhancing drugs and why athletes feel compelled to use, we spent time on desirable alternatives to drug use and how students and athletes can improve and perform at a high level on their own without external aid. In the mid-1990s, we brought Dr. Tutko to Aspen HS address these issues with student athletes, teachers, coaches, and parents. During this time, besides confronting drug use by students, he talked about skills and mindsets students needed to incrementally improve and how parents, teachers, and coaches can enable and/or teach these skills. In the end, he provided an extensive list of characteristics/skills that are crucial for a student-athlete's success and I contend these same skills apply equally to students who are not also athletes. Here are five key skills Tutko identified in his research:

(1) On a Mission. Students who demonstrate this skill know why they are playing, why they are in school, and what the probable results should be. They realize that mission guides a process toward a result, using it like a compass guides them, keeping them true to the vision and direction of their endeavors.

Successful students understand that goals drive their progress toward the completion of the mission and provide the energy which helps to get beyond procrastination and temporary setbacks. Goals are specific, measurable, achievable, and timely; this means you cannot simply say you want to 'get better grades.' Instead, you must identify the specific outcome that is doable and the time frame to accomplish it. Progress toward goals is enabled by objectives, which are the specific steps you take or things you do to reach or achieve what it is you want to do. Objectives are accomplished through strategies, which are the longer-term techniques and methods you employ in those activities or steps. Tactics are the day-to-day and situation-to-situation adjustments you make in the way you execute those strategies as you go along.

(2) Work Hard. These students have a tenacity that is visible and palpable and are willing to simply work harder than most other people. I talked about this idea previously when I clarified the professor's admonition to 'work harder.' Hard work is what you exhibit when you adhere to a routine or schedule of activities related to your goals, objectives, and strategies and culminates in something that very closely resembles a talented, smart, intelligent, and successful student.

(3) Confident and Assertive. These students have a belief, because of their work ethic and tenacity, that it is okay to take on uncomfortable tasks and challenging assignments. A confident student is not afraid to fail because he/she knows the process is supposed to be difficult and any temporary failure is about the event not them as a person. Assertive students are not afraid to exercise their right, even responsibility, to do what they are supposed to do rather than act passively. Assertive students ask questions, sit near the front, offer comments on assigned readings, purposefully engage in regular study sessions, pursue goals and passions, and do what others might not necessarily be willing to do. These types of students work to bring out the best in themselves and their teammates, recognizing that success is a function of growth and self-improvement. Students who are confident and assertive are demonstrating a skill found in leaders.

While it seems a majority of people think only the chosen few can be a leader, when you understand and learn the skills demonstrated by Neal, you too can be a successful leader. To make this point, I shared with the players this quote by John Ryan: "If you live in a culture where [people around you] believe you can be a leader and help you develop the skill you need, you will enthusiastically embrace the mantle of leadership. It might not be your goal to become a CEO or a top politician, but, regardless of your occupation, you will view yourself as a leader at home, at work, and in your community. [However,] if you live in a culture that assumes leadership is not for everyone, that leadership is dependent on whether you have innate leadership skills, and that leadership is defined by your job title rather than your actions, you will have an entirely different view. Unfortunately, that's the culture that most of us live in."

The problem with adopting the 'other person is the leader' position is you will inevitably find yourself in a position requiring action; maybe you will be by yourself or maybe with others, all of whom are waiting for someone to lead. What matters is the mindset where you believe that it is, in fact, possible to grow into someone who is a leader, that it is possible to learn those skills and put them into action if needed. Once you have adopted that growth mindset, it is a matter of education.

John Maxwell is a leadership guru in Atlanta whom I follow and whose work I read. In his book *21 Irrefutable Laws of Leadership*, he argues all leadership is a function of skills which you first demonstrate in personal leadership and any success you might have will be limited by what he calls the "Law of the Lid," with the 'lid' being a lack of these skills. The only way to truly maximize your personal effectiveness and, by extension, the effectiveness of any team of which you are member, is to develop these leadership skills. Indeed, he says talent is not enough to enable success; you can only be as effective as your own leadership skills. You can work hard to be effective, but without these skills, that hard work is likely wasted.

You are constantly put into situations where you are the only person who can solve a problem, where you must *lead yourself*. And once you are able to lead yourself to a solution or through a series of objectives which lead you to a goal, you will be able to lead others, even if you do not have the official title endowing leadership status.

(4). Attentive. Successful students demonstrate a willingness to listen and learn and are able to focus on the task at hand while keeping distractions at bay. The crucial attribute of being in the present, a complete awareness of the absolute necessity of being in the moment, was a key skill discussed earlier in reflection on the lessons presented in the story about Neal's experience on Everest.

(5) Positive expectation. These students believe that the effort, work, and embrace of the process will lead to success, so they walk into each class, practice, study session, and game with a positive expectation that they will perform at their highest level and that the results will reflect that preparation. A mindset of positive expectation does not ignore or overlook the lessons of failure, but instead utilizes those lessons to move toward a better result. What results is a far less stressful experience, which in itself enhances performance. The positive expectation effectively limits negative thought from interfering with the task at hand.

Essentially, Tutko's research and ideas from over 20 years ago and Maxwell's thoughts on leadership have provided a framework for books, articles, and further studies which offer insights on success, effective leadership, toughness, and how to handle adversity.

One topic getting a lot of traction is the idea that educators should teach students skills in toughness. The ability to stick to it regardless of setbacks, to keep your resolve when things are not going your way, is a skill you need to be successful. Toughness is not a posture; it is not how tough you look, act, or speak. It is not how much you can lift in the weight room, how menacing your voice might sound, or the number or location of your tattoos. My own short definition of toughness is a willingness to do what needs to be done when it has to be done, under any time constraint, no matter how uncomfortable you are, without complaining.

A book I have shared and discussed with my business students is called *Fish*, which is a short, fictional story summarizing the secrets to success of the very real Pike Place Fish Market. Authors Steve Lundin and John Christensen talk about the keys to improved results based on Christensen's observations of the fishmongers at Pike Place. He became interested in their toughness, their willingness to perform a stinky, cold, almost dreary job at a very high level. Quite simply, these fishmongers chose to change their attitudes and embrace fun as a way to improve their own experience as well as that of the customers.

If you visit, you will notice that Pike Place Fish Market is not the only fish market in that market; there are at least two others, yet the Pike Place Fish Market is different as evidenced by an almost constant crowd of observers watching the workers throw fish and involving the customers. Directed toward employees and managers as a way to motivate the employees to perform at a higher level and provide top notch customer service, the book focuses on these key components to the 'Fish Philosophy.' Choose your attitude, make their (the customer's) day, have fun, and be present. The prescription for improved results by Lundin and Christensen included the necessity to be present, which served Neal Beidleman and is a key component of Bilas' definition of toughness.

In *Toughness: Developing True Strength on and off the Court*, former Duke basketball player and current ESPN analyst Jay Bilas says that we are not born tough, but rather toughness is a skill that is learned and developed. "Toughness is not physical. It has nothing to do with size, strength, or athleticism. It is an intangible, an attitude, a philosophy… it's a skill that can be developed and improved in everyone." So, toughness goes hand in hand with a growth mindset.

The idea that a process orientation rather than a fixed focus on results, scores, and answers will lead to a better outcome is related to this idea of toughness, which includes the characteristics of persistence, commitment, and resilience. While Bilas is primarily discussing athletic success, I think his advice pertains to academic success as well. Achieving success requires belief in a common goal, belief in yourself, an ability to handle adversity, a willingness to take things one step at a time, recognition that every step in the process is important and worthy of our full attention, a willingness to prepare, an ability to handle criticism, courage, and trust.

How do you develop the skill of toughness? Bilas says that 'no player ever got better just be getting through something. True toughness is competing… after you have prepared yourself mentally to compete.'

Preparation is the investment that enables toughness, as I pointed out in the opening story. The opponent, the competition, the exam doesn't matter. All that matters is your preparation; when you are fully prepared, you can go out and perform "with a high expectancy of success. Preparation is not about talent; those with the most talent feel they can rely on that talent, and may not feel they need to prepare as diligently." While preparation enables toughness, Bilas says commitment, which is measured in the effort and work you are willing to put in, is the key building block for preparation. Being committed means "showing up, prepared to compete and perform at the highest level possible."

Inevitably, when you compete in any endeavor, despite your preparation, commitment, and toughness, things will not go your way. This is adversity, and it is a normal part of life. How do you best handle it?

In his book *Adversity Quotient: Turning Obstacles into Opportunities*, Paul Stoltz, PhD, says that no matter how many games you win, or how successful you have become, you will always experience adversity. Adversity is defined as a difficult situation or a condition marked by distress; calamity or unfavorable fortune. I read a quote by an unattributed coach who said 'adversity is an opportunity to better understand yourself.' The key to handling that situation that has gone against you in a way in which you learn and grow is to embrace a process he calls LEAD.

L stands for Listen to your internal response and contain (stop) the irrational response to an event.

E stands for explore the alternatives, get the entire picture, and figure out what factors you have and/or can take responsibility for fixing.

A stands for analyze the evidence, which includes confronting the assumptions revealed in your initial internal response.

D stands for Do, which is an action you take to gain control of the situation and to disprove those assumptions revealed earlier.

In the end, the success we achieve depends a great deal on the answer to these questions: How do we handle setbacks? What do we do next after a mistake? What are we going to do to solve the problem?

The cliché says winners don't quit and quitters don't win. Indeed, Stoltz says quitters often give up in the face of adversity. Once you quit, you have failed in that endeavor. So, the key is to keep going, embracing the characteristics from Tutko and Bilas and Stoltz. But in every endeavor you undertake, there is, almost necessarily, feedback and criticism. Some of this criticism will be constructive, yet some will be perceived as negative, and some will be hurtful. How you handle that criticism needs to be part of the skill set enabling your success.

Because criticism is a necessary and customary part of the academic (and athletic) endeavor, you must learn to deal with it and the easiest way to do this is to see criticism as desirable feedback that you need in order to improve. The reason I have included a discussion in this section is because so many students see criticism as a form of adversity to be avoided.

I am an advocate for positive coaching, as it reduces your anxiety and a student (and athlete as the case might be) will perform better when he/she is experiencing less anxiety. But even positive coaching requires the professor/teacher to provide honest feedback regarding your progress. Usually, these professionals work hard to frame the feedback in a positive way, but the problem is that even positive feedback is often seen negatively. And even if advocates initiated a motivation program requiring a coach to make you feel better about yourself, Stolz found happy, positive people experience as much adversity as anyone else. He says how the coach, or professor, or teacher makes you feel has very little to do with your success.

In his book *Raising a Team Player*, Harry Sheehy talks to parents about what it takes to be a team player and what parents can do to help their child become a better athlete and teammate, and subsequently how their child can better help his/her team to be successful. Of applicability to students in this context, he wrote specifically about criticism and how to deal with it.

Sheehy tells about an interaction he overheard between a softball player and her coach at Williams College, during his time as athletic director. Evidently, a player had missed a sign from her third base coach, resulting in an out or some sort of negative outcome. The coach called his player over and explained, within earshot of Sheehy, how she had evidently missed the sign, the negative consequences of that one 'miss' and about the need to pay attention to every sign.

Sheehy was very impressed with the calm, emotionless, poised and positive way the coach communicated this to the player. Later he overheard this same player tell her teammates that 'the coach sure did yell at me about that missed sign.' He goes on to talk about how, when he was the highly successful head basketball coach, his own players at Williams College complained about his 'negative' coaching style in their annual evaluation.

Coach Sheehy was dumbfounded by this revelation, as he considered himself one of the most positive coaches he knew. So, the next season, he had his managers chart everything he said as "teaching" statement [sometimes called neutral critical], "positive," "negative criticism," or a "neutral" statement [also could be neutral critical]. The results of that charting process revealed a ratio of positive or teaching statement to negative criticism of 10 to 1. But the players thought exactly the opposite; evidently the players considered the neutral statements to be negative as well which then outweighed the positive in their minds by 10 to 1. It seems to me that he must have had to spend several sessions simply talking about the nature of criticism, the difference between positive, negative, and neutral, and explaining to his athletes how to best transform that criticism into growth.

Criticism, whether you believe it to be positive or negative, is simply feedback on your performance and is valuable because it generally is intended to help you to improve. But beware criticism by another who wants to detract from your mission, your school, your team, your class, or your professor. While you can discount this destructive criticism from outsiders, feedback from your superior, professor, coach, advisor, mentor, teacher or even a more experienced peer is almost always necessary and worthwhile and needs to be heeded. Indeed, feedback received when your coach breaks down tape of your performance, or your teacher comments on a marked paper or returned exam is about the most valuable outcome of any activity as you strive to get better.

Unfortunately, many students don't like any sort of criticism even though coaches and teachers must judge your level of knowledge, skill, talent and play. The misconception that criticism by coaches and teachers is something negative has its roots in a misunderstanding of authority.

In the book *Authority,* authors Eugene Kennedy and Sara Charles discuss the concept of authority and argue that it is one of the most misunderstood concepts in the U.S. We see people in positions of authority leading in authoritarian ways, rather than authoritatively, and we start to think the two are the same. And when criticism comes from the authoritarian leader, it is generally not well received and we begin to think everyone in authority is the same.

They explain in their book the difference between authority/authoritative leaders and authoritarianism. "Authority does not, as does authoritarianism, restrict, control, or repress human development through force, techniques, of manipulation, shaming, or impersonal or whimsical regulations. Authority's whole purpose (and most coaches, but certainly not all, are authoritative rather than authoritarian) is to promote the achievement by its subjects of their goal of full growth."

Sheehy provides a key point regarding the efficacy of criticism. For it to be helpful, criticism must be directed at the behavior not at the person. Most coaches and teachers know the difference and will address the behavior or action. The problem arises when the athlete conflates the coach's or teacher's communication as a personal attack, rather than behavior, driven simply because the coach or professor is talking to him/her personally.

Coach Dawn Reed, head volleyball coach at Beloit College, says everyone regardless of their perceived status, attained degree, honors in high school, outside recognition, position, coverage by the press, or placement in the class can improve through criticism and to that end she says the best thing you can do when receiving any feedback is to swallow your pride. She says, if you say "I know" before the coach, advisor, or professor can finish his/her sentence, you have a pride problem. Listen to those with experience and be respectful of those who have gone before, who have the expertise you probably don't.

Author Gretchen Rubin argues that handling criticism is a necessary universal skill for everyone. She advises you to avoid any sort of defensive reaction in the face of feedback. And if you are criticized for a mistake, she says you should admit it; this enables you (and anyone else involved) to relax and focus on what needs to be done, which enables you to learn from the mistake.

Embrace every component or characteristic of success discussed in this chapter. Each is a skill, technique, or strategy which you can learn and as you put into play each skill, any subsequent action becomes easier. Finally, you get to the point you have assimilated the skill set into your behavior and you react intuitively.

Conclusion

Success is the evidence of improvement over time, not just the score, the win or loss. In any endeavor, things will either work out the way you would like, or not. Generally, if an endeavor you undertake works out the way you would like, it feels good and you feel like a success. If the actions you take don't work out the way you would like, you generally don't feel that good about things, and you feel like you failed. Success is the ability to keep at it despite the setback, to look at the reasons for the result you did not like and to make adjustments which might help you get to the result you would like.

I think we get caught up on the idea of failure as an undesirable end, a final outcome. But failure is part of the process as well. Of course, there are situations where failure is fatal, as in the story about Everest that opened the chapter. But we must remember the vast majority of 'failures' are not fatal, but rather temporary setbacks that seem like failure.

I do not think the loser of an athletic competition or a student who gets an undesirable score in class is a failure, for if that is the case, then why even try? Of course, I have seen many students who are so afraid of failure that they simply quit to find an easier class or major or job outside of academia, something at which they can 'win.' So they win, but are they really successful? I would say no, but since any idea of success has to be internalized, it is unfair for me to judge. I argue that the pursuit of success is a worthwhile endeavor and have tried – in this chapter – to teach you the specific characteristics and skills which successful students possess.

Observation suggests most of us are competitive by nature; we strive to win in sports, and those with a growth mindset strive to attain the highest scores possible in academics. Winning and losing are symbiotic components of that competitive process. Losing forces you to adjust and move on. But the same thing happens when you win; if you stand still, if you don't adjust and grow, you will probably see the less desirable outcome next time. So, whether you win or lose, it is in your best interest to respond to each the same way regardless of the result. After a win, celebrate then analyze the reason why, using that information to grow; after a loss, mourn for a short while then grasp the chance to grow, using the result to provide a lesson for your next endeavor, whether it be an athletic competition or an academic assessment or assignment. Your goal is to be better than you were yesterday.

It is a normal part of the educational and/or athletic process to experience some setbacks. I think the most difficult part is keeping losses in perspective in a society which recognizes, almost demands, a winner. When you strive to achieve anything, you will see some results which are not necessarily what you had in mind. How you respond determines whether it is a failure or just a loss from which you move on. A misconception arising from our adulation of all things successful is the tendency to think that success comes out of nowhere, with little effort, to only a favored few. Inherent in that misperception is the idea some people are talented, some are not, and it is talent which drives all success.

Of course, in almost every case, success happens over hours, days, months, or years of preparation. Success is a process that does not occur in a smooth upward incline, but rather in a series of fits and starts, failed attempts, and successful results followed by further movement toward the goal in a pattern that more resembles a mountain range, with peaks you ascend followed by valleys you have to work through, followed by another mountain range. It is a daunting challenge when you endeavor to be successful. Pick almost any success story, and when you look into the rest of the story you will find someone who has put in play many, if not all, of the characteristics and definitions discussed here.

So huddle up. Things are not supposed to be easy. Education is a struggle; clearly not on the same magnitude of the Everest expedition, but difficult nevertheless. Once you embrace that struggle, you can deal with it, and be successful. Hands in: Toughness on three. 1, 2, 3...

This chapter concludes the collection of skills and strategies which I have presented in an effort to help improve your academic skills infrastructure. Everything in this book is something I have used myself in my own educational endeavors, or accumulated over the years as teacher and coach, or learned in professional development to be taught to my students in the classroom, or shared with student athletes when I was an academic support coach.

The final chapter is a discussion of the Academic Weight Room idea, intended for advisors, advocates, parents, and coaches who would like to put these lessons into practice in the same way I did in my own teaching, coaching, and advising.

Chapter 20
Putting The Academic Weight Room into Action

How and Why: Information for Advocates, Advisors, and Academic Coaches

"…where the young men he recruits have often been raised by mothers and grandmothers and where they will arrive at the school where he coaches with little preparation for the academic work expected of them. These aren't stereotypes, these are the facts…"
Michael Croley

Background Story

I crossed paths with a former student who had done very well in my IB Economics course and who had recently graduated from university. Early on in her time there, one of her required courses was microeconomics during which she first met her now-husband. At a recent holiday office party, she introduced me to him and he shared with me that, for this course, she seemed to be much more advanced than most of the other students; she was one of the 'smart' students.

He thought it was just the economics she had learned in high school and I am sure that was part of her success. But after he spent time on the course, he discovered the key was not just the economics knowledge she exhibited but rather the academic skills she learned previously, much of which occurred in my classroom. While he was an honor student in high school, he found that university work had very little in common with what he had been required to do in high school. He told me that he simply had no idea he was insufficient in the academic skills his wife taught him; he give her all the credit for enabling him to achieve at a much higher level. I appreciate her nod to me, but what the story tells me is that even students who enter university with scores worthy of honor status sometimes find themselves with an academic infrastructure deficiency.

History

We were flying home from an extended visit to Europe when my wife casually mentioned that it was so nice to not have a knot in her stomach… something that typically accompanied normal preparations for the upcoming school year. She had retired in May while I decided to teach one more year.

But that innocent comment initiated a cascade of doubt regarding my decision; there seemed to be some sort of cosmic interference unleashed by a total removal from all things 'education' that the vacation provided. After weeks of agonizing internal debate about whether I should stay (or go) for one more year in the classroom, I decided to submit my resignation.

Post resignation, a few weeks of bike riding and casual conversation over coffee enabled me to ponder the retirement gig in front of me. Oh, the plans I had! But that carefree wonder was interrupted by a call from the Associate Athletic Director at California State, Bakersfield, who said that she had heard from Coach Barnes, for whom my son Jeff is an assistant men's basketball coach, that I might be available for a temporary, part-time position in academic support for athletics at the university. Evidently, the person in charge of the athletics academic support at CSUB had, on relatively short notice, moved on to a different school.

As they were in a slight bind, time-wise, she asked me to submit a proposal for my vision of an academic support program at CSUB, to enable them to get the school year underway and to establish protocols as they searched for a permanent, full-time director. She emailed me the requirements for the proposal, and within a few days I had put together an outline of my vision, mission, goals, objectives, and strategies for what I knew to be a job that would last only a short time. Essentially, my job would be to help move the department forward while creating a culture of academic success that would enable the subsequent director to remode: rather than rebuild the academic support program.

To be clear, I responded to this request for a proposal from a secondary education perspective. Although I had one year of experience as a graduate assistant in academic advising at Northern Arizona University, my proposal would be what I thought it should look like from a teacher/coach perspective rather than what it might look like if it came from someone already in the university advising community.

As a result, while it contained many of the same components that are common in every athletic support department, a key difference was my idea of the Academic Weight Room, which holds that an individual student can improve/develop his or her own academic skills infrastructure. This individualized approach, driven at least partly by a creative effort to maximize relatively limited resources made available for athletics academic support, emphasized self-efficacy and a focus on the process and structure of learning as the path toward academic achievement. Because we had a fiduciary responsibility to stay within the confines of limited resources, I set a goal to reduce tutor utilization while improving academic performance, both of which we accomplished. In addition to the 'normal' athletics academic components of supervised study halls, tutors, and individual appointments for the at-risk athletes, I taught specific academic skills to individual students as well as entire teams and other groups in lectures of 20 to 60 minutes.

Former university athletics academic advisor Phyllis Wallace was offered the other temporary part time position and together we were able to commit human capital that far surpassed the 1.0 FTE funding the university had available when we were hired. We provided the university with over a half-century of experience in education.

Eventually, the funding solidified and the success of the program enabled more resources to be allocated. As a result, the university moved us both to permanent positions with an increase in pay and after a nationwide search, hired a permanent full-time Athletics Academic Services Director. So, within two years, the program moved to solid ground, arguably successfully and innovatively. The administration did everything possible to allow us to do our job, supporting us as we worked to put the athletics academic support center in a position where it had a chance to see some success.

It appears that our relative success at CSUB is seen as an anomaly rather than a possible model. It is also possible that the whole idea of an academic skills infrastructure intervention for at-risk student athletes seems so simple that it could not possibly return the results I submit. After all, if it worked, how come nobody has done this before? I submit that the Academic Weight Room, which focuses on process rather than results, which teaches specific academic skills and routines to students in a group or by academic advisor in a personal appointment with that athlete, can provide the solid academic skill set which the top third of the students seem to have and take for granted.

Why

The quote by Michael Croley at the top of this chapter comes from a story about the life of an assistant basketball coach and while it is an interesting read which provides insight into the Division 1 basketball industry, the important point for my project is the part about "little preparation for the academic work expected of them." They have been admitted to the school but have found it to be a tough slog.

Many of these students are struggling just to stay in school; others are getting by but are at risk of failing. Others wonder if their course difficulties are an indication they might not be smart enough.

Everyone has to remember that in every case in which a student finds herself/himself struggling, she/he has qualified for admission. It is important to recognize that almost every student finds university to be a struggle, at least initially, and the same thing occurs for those going on for their Master's or Doctorate. But some find it more daunting than most. I don't think it's an intelligence or ability issue, but rather technical capabilities which can be taught.

Not all students have ineffective or inefficient academic skills, but my observation is that some students have either not been taught how to learn efficiently and effectively or they have not retained those skills which were once taught to them. Conversations with current teachers suggest that my impression is slowly changing, but I think, generally, that most high school content-area teachers do not teach the process of learning, but rather focus on content in their own discipline. It seems what was once an integral part of the education process has given way to more pressing demands of test scores.

Of course, introductory courses at the high school level and remedial courses at the postsecondary level are designed to teach process more than content, but as the student progresses into more specific content areas, it is less likely he/she will get instruction in the general process. Still, I think that most students have figured out coping strategies and the best students have adopted, assimilated, or learned (in some way) the techniques which allow them to achieve at high levels.

But, across the board, there are students at the high school and university level who exhibit an academic skills infrastructure deficit. And this deficiency should not disqualify them from matriculation when it can be strengthened by teaching specific academic skills.

Anecdotal evidence suggest that roughly one third of the athletes at CSUB were good to excellent students and I hardly ever saw them, nor heard about them from professors, nor were they participants in my workshops. While these students were generally recognized to be scholar athletes as evidenced by an above 3.0 GPA, only a small percentage of these better students were truly at the 'scholar' level, as evidenced by the honors program or national academic recognition such as Rhodes Scholar or Fulbright candidates. The middle third hovered in the average grade range, finding some classes easier than others, but occasionally needing academic support. The bottom third, upon which I focused my time, simply lacked many of these academic skills and were often struggling to make sense of at least one course per term, and sometimes the whole purpose of higher education. And contrary to popular opinion/folklore, these athletes were not 'dumb' nor were they 'lazy.' To the contrary, research indicates that athletes often have superior neurotransmitter pathways than non-athletes and are indeed smart in many ways.

The problem is, for whatever reason, they have not embedded and actualized the 'intelligence' associated with academic success; either no one ever taught them the basic skills and processes required in learning or else they failed to learn what the point of the lesson was at the time it was being taught. For example, it is very likely that a student was taught the research paper process in high school. But it is also possible that the student was more focused on getting the research paper 'done' with a 'good' grade than he/she was interested in the real purpose of the assignment. The point of the research paper was to teach the process, but the student might have interpreted the point to be learning more about the topic about which he/she was writing. Or perhaps, even more likely, the student saw the research paper as busy work that just needed to be completed and assimilated neither result.

The default model at both the high school and university level is for these students in the middle and lower percentiles to engage with tutors who are generally able to help the student improve their performance and scores in a particular class. Using a tutor to get a passing grade in a course, or a 'good' score on an exam, might enable a desirable result. But sometimes, tutoring is not enough. The Academic Weight Room strives for a longer-lasting transformation in the student, one that shifts the focus from the tutor and the result to one of improved academic skill and improved self-efficacy, enabling the student to handle any problem, question, or assignment without that tutor.

How

A parent of a former student recently asked what I have been doing since I retired. I talked about the two years at CSUB and mentioned the Academic Weight Room project on which I have been spending significant time lately. His daughter was a D1 soccer player at a prestigious public university and he offered, as a sort of verification of the inadequate academic preparation of some our athletes, that in a math class at her school she was asked by the professor to help a football player 'get through the class.' Her reply was that she did not think she could really offer much help.

The problem was not only that the player had inadequate content knowledge in math, but he also had serious deficiencies in structural academic skills which really limited her options. The parent's question, one which I cannot answer, was this: 'How did this athlete even get into college?' This issue for the school as well as the athletic department and the coach is that the student is admitted, but underprepared. And it might not even be the student's fault. Who knows what academic skills were even taught during his high school education? The better question, then, is how do we best help these types of students see academic success?

Indeed, it is our job as academic advisors and advocates to help these students to be as successful as possible. The strategy of enhancing self-efficacy by moving the student away from tutoring as the sole path to academic success is detailed in the lessons in this book. Organized in much the same was as my basketball practices were, these 20- to 80-minute sessions taught the students academic skills, rather than content from specific courses and differed from the freshman readiness courses (one of which I taught while I was a graduate assistant) in that each session not only told the student 'what' they needed to be doing, but also how and when. Students can improve their academic skills infrastructure, regardless of its condition and as their advisor, advocate, coach, and teacher, you can use the strategies and techniques offered in this book to help make that happen.

Indeed, I have endeavored to distill academic skills, strategies, or concepts into an essence which can be taught using the IDEA model which is the most common way an athletic coach teaches a scout, game plan, practice plan, drills or offensive strategies.

You will find each chapter of this book presenting strategies and skills in a similar way to what I did in my position as academic support coach, which was to introduce the skill or strategy by

- telling a relevant story so individuals could understand why the skill is beneficial,

- demonstrating what I was talking about by showing them either in a notebook or on the whiteboard so they could understand what the skill is

- providing a detailed explanation of how to do that particular skill, for which I used a PowerPoint for each lesson* to provide visual reinforcement. (*available at www.academicweightroom.com)

I was then able to attend to their practice during required study sessions during which I (and other advisors) monitored their progress. Completing this four-step skill-teaching process removes any doubt regarding the what; there simply is no misunderstanding when the coach not only demonstrates what the skill looks like, but also explains how to do it.

As an advocate for the student(s) you work with, you too can teach the skills I have detailed in this book. When you earn their trust by developing an authentic, caring relationship with high expectations, they will put effort into their own skill development. I have found most students are smart and capable, so do not minimize their ability to succeed and achieve at a higher level.

The expectations you have are driven by the vision for this project: 'Process is intelligence getting to know itself.' The vision drives the mission which ensures you stay the course, that you see the value in continuing your advocacy of their growth: 'every student can improve his/her academic skills infrastructure.'

The goals, represented by the chapters in this book, are what enables both you and the student to fulfill that mission. These goals represent the specific skills necessary for not only academic success, but success in the student's endeavors after university. Objectives are the steps taken to reach the goal, and these are detailed in the explanation provided in each chapter.

Embrace the vision, mission, goals, and objectives of the Academic Weight Room project and your student(s) can improve their academic skill infrastructure.

Final Thought

An acquaintance asked me what specific teaching tool was most effective in helping these advisees become better students, and/or to better engage in their own specific course. Of course, all of the techniques and strategies enhanced their overall academic skill and enabled them to become smarter. But she wanted to know about techniques a teacher might use, outside of what is covered in the book.

The situation I encountered most often was surprisingly common for university students. Many students I worked with had difficulty getting started on an essay, or interpreting a reading, or writing a speech, or formulating an argument. They would sit there, appearing clueless, evidently waiting for prompts, maybe even answers to direct their writing, analysis, or interpretation. The technique which worked every time to help the student unlock their own thinking was for me to record their own words and thoughts. I told them to just start talking about the assignment, and then I wrote down, usually on the whiteboard, everything they said. If they were so stuck that thoughts were not forthcoming, I utilized questions to get them thinking about the assignment: What? Why? Where? When? How?

Once their own words and thoughts were visible on the board, or paper as might have been the case, they were able to organize them into whatever structure was necessary. Once they saw the nature of this process after a few sessions, most were able to do this 'thinking out loud' exercise on their own.

Let's Do This

When I talk to people about this project, a common response is something similar to this: "Oh, like study skills."

Well, sort of.

This book is about how students can become smarter by improving their academic skills infrastructure. As an advocate for your student(s), you can use this model to plant seeds of change for academic improvement. Their potential is a function of a mindset that growth is possible, rather believing in fixed intelligence.

"We've all long thought the IQ with which you were branded in [primary, middle, or secondary] school after taking one of those aptitude tests was the final word on your intellectual destiny. Not true." So said Dr. Francis E. Jensen, M.D, in his book *The Teenage Brain* in which he discusses how students can indeed become smarter.

Any student already attending, or intending to attend, college or university can learn the skills necessary to be successful. It's not that struggling students are not smart enough, but rather the fact they simply do not know how to do the things smart students are already doing. As I said previously, at least a third and up to a half of all students in post-secondary education are deficient in one or more of the skills included in the academic skills infrastructure. And this academic infrastructure deficiency is not necessarily their own fault. While this is gradually changing, especially in the middle grades, teachers tend to focus on content and tell students what to do without following up with the necessary how and why.

A former colleague who is now teaching math at the community college level had not seen me in a few years and wanted to know what I was doing. After I gave her the three-minute story of my time at CSUB and a summary of the premise of this book, she said, "Wow, there are at least three things I am going to address in my class on Monday. This is exactly what many of them need." You don't have to be a post-secondary teacher to make a difference in a student's life. Anyone who is an advocate, adviser, coach, parent, or teacher can do this. Now is the time to start. Do not let these students down. They can become smarter and you can help.

Okay, huddle up. Embrace the process. Process on three.

One, two, three!

Bibliography

Adams, Scott. *How to Fail at Almost Everything and Still Win Big*. Portfolio/Penguin. New York, NY. 2013

Adler, Mortimer, & Van Doren, Charles. *How to Read a Book*. A Touchstone book by Simon and Schuster. New York, NY. 1972.

AVID for Higher Education. *Charting Text*. California State University, Bakersfield. 2013.

Bain, Ken. *What the Best Teachers Do*. Harvard University Press. Cambridge, MA. 2004.

Bilas, Jay. *Toughness: Developing True Strength On and Off the Court*. New American Library. New York. 2013.

Brown, Peter; Roediger, Henry & McDaniel, Mark. *Make it Stick: The Science of Successful Learning*. Belknap Press of Harvard University Press. Cambridge, MA. 2104

Cathers, Bill. Aspen Institute. Socratic Seminar Shared Inquiry Workshop. Feb 7, 2004. www.cathersconsulting.com

Collins, Christina Hank. *A Guide to Creating Questions for Close Analytical Reading*. turnonyourbrain.wordpress.com

Colvin, Geoff. *Talent is Overrated*. Penguin Group. New York. 2008

Colorado State University. Coursework in support of post-bachelor's certificate in Education. 1975

Bibliography

Croley, Michael. *Keep Moving: The Nomadic Life of an Assistant Basketball Coach*. SBnation. Nov 2014. http://www.sbnation.com/longform/2014/11/12/7193135/keep-moving-the-nomadic-life-of-an-assistant-college-basketball-coach

Crum, Alia. "Change your Mindset, Change the Game", TED Talk. www.youtube.com/watch?v=ev65KnPHVUk

Curwin, Richard. *Telling Isn't Teaching: The Fine Art of Coaching*. www.edutopia.org/blog/telling-isnt-teaching-richard-curwin. April 4, 2012.

Davis, Brian. *To Restore Academic Integrity in Sports, Hold Head Coaches Accountable*. National Athletics Academic Advisors (N4A) listserv, February 9, 2015.

Dweck, Carol. *Mindset: The New Psychology of Success*. Ballantine Books. 1997.

Fripp, Robert. www.dgmlive.com

Gawande, Atul. *Personal Best*. www.newyorker.com/2011/10/03/personal-best

Goldstein, Jeff. Twitter: @doctorjeff. 10/1/15.

Hartshorn, Nick. *Catch: A Discovery of America*. MacMurray and Beck. Denver/Aspen. 1996.

IBO.org. Teacher classroom resources for IB Business and Management and IB Economics.

IBO.org. International Baccalaureate teacher certification workshops: United World College, Las Vegas NM (2000, 2010); St. Clare's College, Oxford, England; King's College, Birmingham, England. 2012

Jackson, Phil. *Sacred Hoops*. Hyperion. New York, NY. 1995.

Jensen, Francis, MD. *The Teenage Brain*. HarperCollins. New York, NY. 2015.

Kennedy, Eugene & Charles, Sara, MD. *Authority: The Most Misunderstood Idea in America*. The Free Press. New York. 1997.

Lamont, Tom. *My Big Fail: Losers Come Clean on their All-Time Low*. The Guardian. March 28, 2015.

Loehr, James & McLaughlin, Peter. *Mentally Tough: The Principles of Winning at Sports Applied to Winning in Business*. M. Evans and Company. New York. 1986.

Lundin, Steve & Christensen, John. *Fish: A Remarkable Way to Boost Morale and Improve Results*. Hyperion. New York, NY. 2000.

Maxwell, John C. *The 21 Irrefutable Laws of Leadership*. Nashville: Thomas Nelson, 1998.

Medina, John. *Brain Rules*. Pear Press. Seattle, WA. 2008.

Miller, Adam. ACM Consulting. *Attracting and Retaining Top Talent*. Toronto Ontario Canada. www.acmconsulting.ca

Morrison, Van. *Enlightenment*. From the album *Enlightenment*. 1990.

Murphy, Shane, PhD. *The Achievement Zone: An 8-Step Guide to Peak Performance in all Areas of Life*. Berkley Books. New York. 1996.

Northern Arizona University. Coursework in support of Master of Arts in Secondary Education. 1986-87.

Oakley, Barbara. *A Mind for Numbers: How to Excel at Math and Science, Even if you Flunked Algebra*. Jeremy P. Tarcher, Penguin Books. New York. 2014.

Bibliography

Olympic Coach, Volume 21, Number 1, pg 4-7. www.teamusa.org

Pink Floyd. *Time*, written by David Gilmour, Roger Waters, Rick Wright, and Nick Mason. From the album *Dark Side of the Moon*. 1973.

Poundstone, William. *Rock Breaks Scissors*. Little Brown and Company. New York, NY. 2014.

Reed, Dawn. Head Coach, Beloit College. http://coachdawnwrites.com/2012/03/how-to-handle-criticism-constructively/

Rubin, Gretchen. @gretchenrubin http://www.gretchenrubin.com/happiness_project/2012/08/7-tips-for-handling-criticism/

Ryan, John. *What's Your Leadership Mindset?* Business Week, June 19, 2009.

Seiter, Courtney. *"The Formula to Better Problem Solving"*. Fast Company. Jan 2015 http://www.fastcompany.com/3040428/the-formula-to-better-problem-solving

Sheehy, Harry. *Raising a Team Player*. Storey Books. North Adams, MA. 2002.

Sinek, Simon. *Start with Why*. Portfolio/Penguin Group. New York, NY. 2009.

Stolz, Paul. *Adversity Quotient: Turning Obstacles into Opportunities*. John Wiley & Sons. New York. 1999.

Strong, Michael. *The Habit of Thought: From Socratic Seminars to Socratic Practice*. New View Publications. Chapel Hill, NC. 1997.

Taleb, Nassim. *Fooled by Randomness.* Random House. New York, NY. 2005.

Tutko, Thomas, PhD. *Sports Psyching: Playing Your Best Game All of the Time.* J. P. Tarcher. Los Angeles. 1976.

Tutko, Thomas, PhD. Lecture at Aspen High School. 1995.

Votsis, Manolis. tweeted via @edutopia. 9/18/15

Wiggins, Grant. *On Close Reading, Part 2.* grantwiggins.wordpress.com 5/17/2013

Wiggins, Grant. *Where Essential Questions Come From.* www.teachthought.com June 1 2013.

Wiley, William. *Questioning Skills for Teachers.* 3rd Edition. National Education Association Professional Library. 1991.

Wong, Harry. *The First Days of School: How to be an Effective Teacher.* Harry Wong Publications. 2005.

Wooden, John & Jamison, Steve. *Wooden.* NTC Contemporary Publishing. Chicago. 1997.

Wrisberg, Craig. *Sport Skill Instruction for Coaches.* Human Kinetics. Champaign IL. 2007.

Vernacchia, Ralph, Ph.D., McGuire, Richard, Ph.D. & Cook, David, Ph.D. *Coaching Mental Excellence.* Brown and Benchmark. Dubuque, IA. 1992.

Other Books from Bennion Kearny

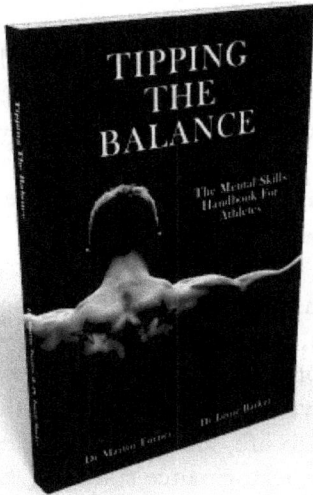

Tipping The Balance: The Mental Skills Handbook For Athletes [Sport Psychology Series] by Martin Turner and Jamie Barker

"The ability to produce a world-beating time is about how you use your mind to allow your body to function with freedom and fluency."

Many athletes grow up with the philosophy that their mental approach to performance is fixed. They do the same things over and over again and expect excellence. But we know that mental approaches are not fixed. They are extremely changeable and adaptable, and therefore the greatest athletes can develop their mental approaches to fulfil their potential. Athletes who can deal with pressure enjoy their sport more, achieve excellence and are resilient to the demands of competition and training.

Tipping The Balance offers contemporary evidence-based and highly practical mental strategies that help an athlete to develop the crucial mental skills that enable them to thrive under pressure, perform consistently when it matters most, and enjoy the challenge of the big event.

This book is about empowering you - the athlete - no matter what level you perform at. In this book you will discover the secrets of how the world's greatest athletes draw on cutting edge psychological skills to use what's between their ears to maximize performance.

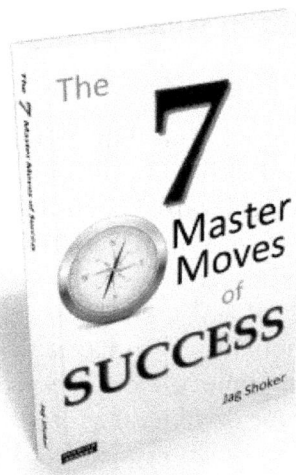

The 7 Master Moves of Success
by Jag Shoker

One of the most common clichés about success - that it is a journey, not a destination - has concealed one of its most defining qualities. Success really is a dynamic and ever-moving process. It is about making the right moves at the right time.

In this absorbing and uplifting book, Jag Shoker – a leading performance coach to business leaders, sports professionals and creative performers – brings the science and inspiration behind success to life. He reveals the 7 Master Moves that combine to create the high performance state that he calls Inspired Movement: the ability to perform an optimal series of moves to create the success you desire most.

Drawing widely on scientific research, his extensive consultancy experiences, and insights into the successes of top performers in business, sport, and entertainment, 7 Master Moves is a synthesis of the leading-edge thinking, and paradigms, that underpin personal performance and potential.

Building upon key research in fields such as neuroscience, psychology, expert performance and talent development - 7 Master Moves represents an evidence-based 'meta' theory of what really works. Compelling to read, and easy to follow, the book incorporates a strong practical element and shares a number of powerful and practical exercises that can help you apply each Master Move and achieve greater results in your life and work.

Regardless of your profession or passion in life, the 7 Master Moves will reward those who are prepared to work hard to achieve the success that matters most to them.